# Mastering KnockoutJS

Use and extend Knockout to deliver feature-rich, modern web applications

**Timothy Moran**

[PACKT] open source *
PUBLISHING
community experience distilled
BIRMINGHAM - MUMBAI

# Mastering KnockoutJS

Copyright © 2014 Packt Publishing

First published: November 2014

Production reference: 1191114

Published by Packt Publishing Ltd.
Livery Place
35 Livery Street
Birmingham B3 2PB, UK.

ISBN 978-1-78398-100-7

www.packtpub.com

# Credits

**Author**
Timothy Moran

**Reviewers**
Michael Best
Peter Himschoot
Anders Malmgren
Viktor Nemes
Julia Rechkunova
Patrick Walters

**Acquisition Editor**
Reshma Raman

**Content Development Editor**
Manasi Pandire

**Technical Editor**
Humera Shaikh

**Copy Editors**
Shambhavi Pai
Stuti Srivastava

**Project Coordinator**
Leena Purkait

**Proofreaders**
Simran Bhogal
Ameesha Green
Paul Hindle

**Indexer**
Tejal Soni

**Graphics**
Sheetal Aute

**Production Coordinator**
Aparna Bhagat

**Cover Work**
Aparna Bhagat

# About the Author

**Timothy Moran** has been working in the field of software for the last 4 years. He started with desktop development for .NET and moved on to web development for a variety of technologies. Timothy began using Knockout shortly after the release of Version 1.3 and has since used it in several projects personally and professionally. He also provides community support by answering questions on StackOverflow.

This is Timothy's first title.

# About the Reviewers

**Peter Himschoot** works as a lead trainer and architect at U2U (www.u2u.net), which is a Microsoft-certified partner for learning solutions based in Brussels, Belgium.

He has a wide interest in software development, including web, Windows, TFS, and mobile applications. Over the last 10 years, he has trained thousands of developers and was involved in many web development projects as a software architect.

**Anders Malmgren** is a committed and driven solutions architect and senior consultant who enjoys working on customer-oriented projects. He has good experience in designing and developing customer-specific IT solutions in .NET and other technologies such as Knockout. He's passionate about continuous learning, reading blogs, and testing new technologies regularly. Anders is currently working at a prominent Agile IT software development company called Agero Ltd.

He's an active member of the community and tries to contribute as much as possible, either through his blog, GitHub, or StackOverflow. You can find him on his blog at andersmalmgren.com or on GitHub at github.com/AndersMalmgren.

**Viktor Nemes** has been working as a professional software developer since 2008. He lives in Hungary and currently works at TechTalk. He is a full stack developer who is constantly going back and forth from the depth of databases through the world of services to client-side tinkering with the UI. He mainly deals with .NET and C# and builds various applications ranging from rich clients using WPF/Silverlight to web applications using different versions of the ASP.NET MVC.

He likes to play with other development stacks such as Ruby and Node.js and with JavaScript in general. His love for the MVVM pattern started in WPF and found its new home in browsers with the help of KnockoutJS.

When he is not spending his spare time with his family, he loves to chase virtual points on sites such as StackOverflow, CodeEval, Kongregate, or anywhere he can find interesting puzzles to solve.

**Julia Rechkunova** is a software engineer who is inspired by web development and design. She has over 4 years of experience and focuses on the quality and usability of web applications. She enjoys working as a frontend and backend developer. Modern web technologies and tools are the best instruments that help her build great applications and make the world better. She graduated with a Master's degree in Computer Science, started working as an HTML5 game developer, and then participated in startups. She has a passion for frontend programming and contributes to open source projects. Currently, she works with technologies such as HTML5, CSS3, JavaScript, Node.js, and other popular frameworks. Julia also likes to create new tools that bring something different to the industry.

**Patrick Walters** is a software enthusiast who has been actively developing various software since a very young age, and he enjoys doing so professionally. He has worn many hats in his career and loves the creative aspect of developing and teaching others.

He has been actively developing KnockoutJS applications for several years and enjoys writing about them and other open source technologies on his blog at `patrickwalters.net`; he can also be found on Twitter at @pwkad.

# www.PacktPub.com

## Support files, eBooks, discount offers, and more

For support files and downloads related to your book, please visit www.PacktPub.com.

Did you know that Packt offers eBook versions of every book published, with PDF and ePub files available? You can upgrade to the eBook version at www.PacktPub.com and as a print book customer, you are entitled to a discount on the eBook copy. Get in touch with us at service@packtpub.com for more details.

At www.PacktPub.com, you can also read a collection of free technical articles, sign up for a range of free newsletters and receive exclusive discounts and offers on Packt books and eBooks.

https://www2.packtpub.com/books/subscription/packtlib

Do you need instant solutions to your IT questions? PacktLib is Packt's online digital book library. Here, you can search, access, and read Packt's entire library of books.

## Why subscribe?

- Fully searchable across every book published by Packt
- Copy and paste, print, and bookmark content
- On demand and accessible via a web browser

## Free access for Packt account holders

If you have an account with Packt at www.PacktPub.com, you can use this to access PacktLib today and view 9 entirely free books. Simply use your login credentials for immediate access.

# Table of Contents

# Preface

Knockout is built around a pattern that started in Microsoft. This model is Model-View-ViewModel (MVVM), and I think introducing this pattern to newcomers is one of the biggest obstacles to wider adoption. Nearly every other JavaScript library or framework, along with most server-side frameworks, has been built around the Model-View-Controller (MVC) pattern, and the differences between the two are sometimes confusing, even for experienced developers. This problem is compounded by the fact that some larger frameworks, such as AngularJS, end up with a pattern that is nearly identical to MVVM.

Knockout's documentation is excellent, and its live examples and interactive tutorials are some of the best. When it comes to organizing full applications, though, more explanation is required. When I started writing this book, there was only one book on Knockout on Amazon, and it didn't have very favorable reviews. It seemed like a complete guide to using Knockout as the central piece of a frontend stack was missing.

I have been using Knockout for 3 years now, and I've been an active member of the community on StackOverflow and GitHub for 2 years. I've used Knockout in several professional applications as well as a dozen or so personal projects. It is, by far, my favorite JavaScript library, and I strongly prefer MVVM over MVC for developing client applications. Hopefully, you feel that this book gives you everything you need in order to be successful with Knockout.

## A note on Knockout 3.2

Knockout 3.2 was released while this book was being written. *Chapter 4, Application Development with Components and Modules*, was rewritten to include the components feature, and some minor changes were made to other chapters in order to make them accurate. However, most of the code samples were written against Knockout 3.1, and so they do not take advantage of pure computed observables or other features that were released in Knockout 3.2.

# What this book covers

*Chapter 1, Knockout Essentials*, covers the environment setup and basic use of the Knockout library. It also covers data binding, observables, binding handlers, and extenders, and demonstrates a simple Knockout Contacts List application.

*Chapter 2, Extending Knockout with Custom Binding Handlers*, gives you in-depth knowledge of how to create and use custom binding handlers. It includes simple single-property binding handlers as well as complex multiproperty binding handlers with templates.

*Chapter 3, Extending Knockout with Preprocessors and Providers*, teaches you how to use node and binding preprocessors and binding providers to customize Knockout's syntax. It also explores the Knockout Punches library.

*Chapter 4, Application Development with Components and Modules*, explains how to use RequireJS Asynchronous Module Definitions (AMDs) with Knockout to create organized, modular viewmodels. It also teaches you how to use the new Knockout components feature and how to continue working with the Contacts List demo application.

*Chapter 5, Durandal – the Knockout Framework*, explores the basics of the Knockout-based Durandal framework. This chapter covers composition, routing, modal dialogs, and custom widgets.

*Chapter 6, Advanced Durandal*, continues looking at the use of the Durandal framework. This chapter covers events, advanced composition, nested routers, custom dialogs, and the observable plugin.

*Chapter 7, Best Practices*, takes a deep dive into the inner workings of Knockout. It includes dependency detection and the publish/subscribe implementation, observable inheritance, the template engine, and a complete Knockout utility (ko.utils) reference.

*Chapter 8, Plugins and Other Knockout Libraries*, gives you an overview of the recommended patterns and practices for Knockout developers.

*Chapter 9, Under the Hood*, covers several popular Knockout plugins, including Knockout validation, Knockout mapping, and the new Knockout-ES5 plugin.

# What you need for this book

You need an ES5-compatible browser, Git, and Node.js. The code in this book will run on any operating system.

# Who this book is for

If you are an experienced JavaScript developer who is looking for new tools to build web applications and gain an understanding of core elements and applications, this is the book for you. It is assumed that you have basic knowledge of DOM, JavaScript, and KnockoutJS.

# Conventions

In this book, you will find a number of styles of text that distinguish between different kinds of information. Here are some examples of these styles, and an explanation of their meaning.

Code words in text, database table names, folder names, filenames, file extensions, pathnames, dummy URLs, user input, and Twitter handles are shown as follows: "All the code needed to start each chapter can be found in a branch named `cp[chapter#]-[sample]`."

A block of code is set as follows:

```
var subtotal = ko.observable(0);
var tax = ko.observable(0.05);
var total = ko.computed(function() {
  var subtotal = parseFloat(self.subtotal()),
  tax = parseFloat(self.tax());
  return subtotal * (1 + tax);
});
```

**New terms** and **important words** are shown in bold. Words that you see on the screen, in menus or dialog boxes for example, appear in the text like this: "You might have noticed in the previous section that when the **Contacts** page view model communicated with the data service, it wasn't dealing with JSON, but real JavaScript objects."

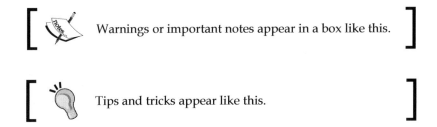

Warnings or important notes appear in a box like this.

Tips and tricks appear like this.

# Reader feedback

Feedback from our readers is always welcome. Let us know what you think about this book—what you liked or may have disliked. Reader feedback is important for us to develop titles that you really get the most out of.

To send us general feedback, simply send an e-mail to feedback@packtpub.com, and mention the book title via the subject of your message.

If there is a topic that you have expertise in and you are interested in either writing or contributing to a book, see our author guide on www.packtpub.com/authors.

# Customer support

Now that you are the proud owner of a Packt book, we have a number of things to help you to get the most from your purchase.

# Downloading the example code

You can download the example code files for all Packt books you have purchased from your account at http://www.packtpub.com. If you purchased this book elsewhere, you can visit http://www.packtpub.com/support and register to have the files e-mailed directly to you.

Additionally, the code for this book is part of a Git repository, which is available on GitHub at https://github.com/tyrsius/MasteringKnockout. The code samples are organized as branches in the repository.

# Errata

Although we have taken every care to ensure the accuracy of our content, mistakes do happen. If you find a mistake in one of our books—maybe a mistake in the text or the code—we would be grateful if you would report this to us. By doing so, you can save other readers from frustration and help us improve subsequent versions of this book. If you find any errata, please report them by visiting http://www.packtpub.com/submit-errata, selecting your book, clicking on the **errata submission form** link, and entering the details of your errata. Once your errata are verified, your submission will be accepted and the errata will be uploaded on our website, or added to any list of existing errata, under the Errata section of that title. Any existing errata can be viewed by selecting your title from http://www.packtpub.com/support.

# Piracy

Piracy of copyright material on the Internet is an ongoing problem across all media. At Packt, we take the protection of our copyright and licenses very seriously. If you come across any illegal copies of our works, in any form, on the Internet, please provide us with the location address or website name immediately so that we can pursue a remedy.

Please contact us at copyright@packtpub.com with a link to the suspected pirated material.

We appreciate your help in protecting our authors, and our ability to bring you valuable content.

# Questions

You can contact us at questions@packtpub.com if you are having a problem with any aspect of the book, and we will do our best to address it.

# 1
# Knockout Essentials

Though it is expected that you have experience with both JavaScript and **KnockoutJS**, we will still be covering the basics to establish a common foundation. This book wouldn't be complete if we didn't cover at least the basics. After that, we will look at building a simple application to create and manage contact information. This application will be used throughout the book to explore new techniques in Knockout and see how they fit into the larger process of application development. In this chapter, you will learn how to:

- Define viewmodels
- Write standard bindings
- Use extenders
- Use templates
- Put all these pieces together into a functional application

This covers most of the standard functionalities in Knockout. In the next chapter, we will look at creating our own bindings to extend Knockout.

Even if you have used Knockout before and don't think you need a refresher, I encourage you to at least read the section that covers the `Contacts List` application example. It's something we will be using throughout the book as we explore more advanced concepts.

Before we get started, let's get our development environment set up.

# The environment setup

We will be using a simple **Node.js** server to host our application because it will run on any operating system. If you haven't done so, install Node.js by following the instructions at `http://nodejs.org/download`.

We will be using **Git** to manage the code for each chapter. If you haven't done so, install Git by following the instructions at `http://git-scm.com/book/en/Getting-Started-Installing-Git`. The code for this book can be downloaded from `http://www.packtpub.com`. All the code needed to start each chapter can be found in a branch named `cp[chapter#]-[sample]`. For example, the first sample we will look at is going to be in the `cp1-computeds` branch.

To begin, clone the repository from `https://github.com/tyrsius/MasteringKnockout`. You can either use the provided download links or run the following command:

```
git clone git@github.com:tyrsius/MasteringKnockout
```

Then, check out the first sample using:

```
git checkout cp1
```

All the examples follow the same pattern. At the root is a `server.js` file that contains a boilerplate Node.js server. Inside the client directory is all the code for the application. To run the application, run this from the command line:

```
node server.js
```

Keep the command-line window open else the server will stop running. Then, open your web browser and navigate to `http://localhost:3000`. If you've set up your environment correctly, you should be looking at the empty `Contacts List` application, as shown in the following screenshot:

The `cp1` branch contains a skeleton with some blank pages. Until we get to the **Contacts** application, most of the samples will not have the **Contacts** or **Settings** pages; they will just present the code on the home page.

# Looking at the samples

Samples of running code are provided throughout the book. They are in branches in the Git repository. You can look at them by checking out the branch, using the following command:

```
git checkout [BranchName]
```

Since the repository is a functional app, most of the code is not relevant to the samples. The `client` directory contains the `index.html` and `shell.html` pages, as well as the `app`, `content`, and `lib` directories. The `app` directory is where our JavaScript is located. The `content` directory contains the included CSS and `lib` contains third-party code (Knockout, jQuery, and Twitter Bootstrap).

The included Node server has a very simple view composition that places the contents of a page in the `{{ body }}` section of the shell. If you have worked with any server-side MVC frameworks, such as Ruby on Rails or ASP.NET MVC, you will be familiar with this. The mechanism is not related to Knockout, but it will help us keep our code separated as we add files. The shell is in the `shell.html` file. You can take a look at it, but it's not directly related to the samples. The HTML for samples is in the `client/index.html` file. The JavaScript for samples is in the `client/app/sample.js` file.

# JavaScript's compatibility

Throughout this book, we will be using code that relies on ECMAScript 5 features, which are supported on all modern browsers. I encourage you to run these examples using a compatible browser. If you cannot, or if you are interested in running them in an older environment, you can use a **polyfill** for them. A polyfill is a JavaScript library that adds standard features to old environments to allow them to run modern code. For the ECMAScript 5 functions, I recommend **Sugar.js**. For the CSS3 media query support, I recommend **Respond.js**.

# An overview of Knockout

Knockout is a library designed for **Model-View-ViewModel (MVVM)** development. This pattern, a descendant of Martin Fowler's Presentation model, encourages the separation of **User Interface (UI)** from the business logic of the domain model. To facilitate this separation, Knockout provides the three necessary components for implementing this pattern, namely, a declarative syntax for the view (the data-bind HTML attribute), a mechanism to notify changes from the viewmodel (the observable object), and a data binder to mediate between the two (Knockout's binding handler).

We will be covering the data-bind and observable object syntax here; the binding handler syntax and its use will be covered in the next chapter.

Using the MVVM pattern means your viewmodel operates on data with JavaScript, and your HTML view is described using the declarative data-binding syntax. Your JavaScript code should not be directly accessing or modifying the view—data-binding should handle that by translating your observable objects into HTML using binding handlers.

The best way to think about the separation between view and viewmodel is to consider whether two different views could use your viewmodel. While this is often not done, it is still helpful to keep it in mind because it forces you to maintain the separation between them. MVVM allows you to redesign the view without affecting the viewmodel.

# Observables

Knockout follows a publish/subscribe pattern to keep data in sync between different parts of the application, such as the UI and the viewmodel. The publisher in Knockout is the observable object. If you've used MVVM before in **Windows Presentation Foundation (WPF)** development, then observable objects can be thought of as Knockout's `INotifyPropertyChanged` implementation.

To construct an observable, the `observable` function is called on the global `ko` object:

```
this.property = ko.observable('default value');
```

The `observable` function returns a new observable. If `ko.observable` is called with a value, it returns an observable with that value.

 The reason why Knockout observables are JavaScript functions instead of normal properties is to allow support for older browsers such as Internet Explorer 6, which did not support getters and setters on properties. Without that ability, setting properties would have no mechanism to notify subscribers about changes.

Observables are JavaScript functions that record subscribers reading their value, then call these subscribers when the value has been changed. This is done using Knockout's dependency tracking mechanism.

Observables are read by calling them without any parameters. To write to an observable, call it with the value as the first and only parameter (further parameters are ignored):

```
var total = vm.total();// read value
vm.total(50);// write new value
```

Observables can contain any legal JavaScript value: primitives, arrays, objects, functions, and even other observables (though this wouldn't be that useful). It doesn't matter what the value is; observables merely provide a mechanism to report when that value has been changed.

# Observable arrays

Though standard observables can contain arrays, they aren't well suited to track changes in them. This is because the observable is looking for changes in the value of the array, a reference to the array itself, which is not affected by adding or removing elements. As this is what most people expect change notification to look like on an array, Knockout provides the observableArray:

```
this.users = ko.observableArray(myUsers);
```

Like observables, arrays can be constructed with an initial value. Normally, you access an observable by calling it or setting its value by passing it a parameter. With observable arrays it's a little different. As the value of the array is its reference, setting that value would change the entire array. Instead, you usually want to operate on the array by adding or removing elements. Consider the following action:

```
this.users().push(new User("Tim"));
```

By calling this.users(), the underlying array is retrieved before a new user is pushed to it. In this case, Knockout is not aware that the array was changed, as the change was made to the array itself and not the observable. To allow Knockout to properly track changes, these changes need to be made to the observable, not the underlying value.

To do this, Knockout provides the standard array methods on the observable, namely, `push`, `pop`, `shift`, `unshift`, `sort`, `reverse`, and `splice`. The call should look like this:

```
this.users.push(new User("Tim"));
```

Notice that instead of retrieving the array from the observable, we are calling `push` directly on the observable. This will ensure that subscribers are notified of the change with an updated array.

# Computed observables

Observables are properties that are set manually, either through your code or by bindings from the UI. Computed observables are properties that automatically update their value by responding to changes in their dependencies, as shown in the following code:

```
var subtotal = ko.observable(0);
var tax = ko.observable(0.05);
var total   = ko.computed(function() {
  return parseFloat(subtotal()) * (1 + parseFloat(tax()));
});
```

In this example, `subtotal` and `tax` are the dependencies of the `total` computed observable. For the first time, the computed observable calculates records of any other observables that were accessed and creates a subscription for them. The result is that whenever `subtotal` or `tax` are changed, the `total` is recalculated and notified to its subscribers. It helps to think of computed observables as declarative values; you define their value as a formula and they will keep themselves up to date.

The `parseFloat` calls are to ensure that they are treated as numbers instead of strings, which would cause concatenation instead of arithmetic. As Knockout binds data against HTML attributes, which are always strings, updates from data binding produce strings. When we discuss extenders, you will see another way to manage this issue.

You can see a sample of this on the `cp1-computeds` branch:

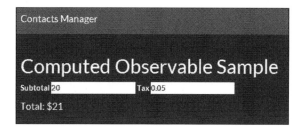

Try changing some of the numbers and watch the `total` computed value update automatically. You can see that the viewmodel code contains just this sample by looking in the `client/app/sample.js` file.

# Writable computed observables

The preceding `total` example is a read-only computed. While they are less common, it is also possible to make a computed observable writable. To do so, pass an object with a `read` and `write` function to `ko.computed`:

```
var subtotal = ko.observable(0);
var tax = ko.observable(0.05);
var total   = ko.computed({
  write: function(newValue) {
      subtotal(newValue / (1 + parseFloat(self.tax())));
  },
  read: function() {
      parseFloat(subtotal()) * (1 + parseFloat(tax()));
  }
});
```

When something attempts to write to the `total` computed now, it will cause the `subtotal` observable to be updated by the `write` function. This is a very powerful technique, but it is not always necessary. In some cases being unable to write directly to `total` might be a good thing, such as when `total` might involve conditionally applying tax to a list of items. You should use writeable computeds only when it makes sense to do so.

You can see an example of this in the `cp1-writecomputed` branch. The `total` computed is now bound to an `input` element such as the `subtotal` and `tax` properties, and changes to the value will reflect back into the `subtotal` observable.

## Pure computed observables

Nonpure computed observables re-evaluate themselves whenever any of their dependencies change, even if there are no subscribers to receive the updated value. This re-evaluation can be useful if the computed also has intentional side effects, but it wastes memory and the processor's cycles if it has no side effects. Pure computed observables, on the other hand, do not re-evaluate when there are no subscribers.

Pure computed observables have two states: **listening** and **sleeping**. When a pure computed has subscribers, it will be listening and behaving exactly like a normal computed. When a pure computed has no subscribers, it will enter its sleeping state and dispose off all of its dependency subscriptions. When it wakes up, the pure computed will re-evaluate itself to ensure its value is correct.

Pure computed observables are useful when a value may go unused for an extended period of time, as they do not re-evaluate. However, since a pure computed always re-evaluates when accessed from a sleeping state, it can sometimes perform worse than a normal computed observable. Since normal computeds only re-evaluate when their dependencies change, a computed observable that is frequently woken from a sleeping state could potentially evaluate its dependencies more often.

There are two ways to create a pure computed: by using `ko.pureComputed` or by passing `{ pure: true }` as the third parameter to `ko.computed`:

```
var total = ko.pureComputed(function() {
  return parseFloat(subtotal()) * (1 + parseFloat(tax())));
});
//OR
var total = ko.computed(function() {
  return parseFloat(subtotal()) * (1 + parseFloat(tax())));
}, this, { pure: true });
```

 Pure computed observables were introduced in Knockout 3.2, which was not released at the time this book was written. None of the code samples take advantage of pure computed observables, even though many of the samples would have benefited from them.

# Manual subscriptions

Sometimes you need to do more than update a dependent value when an observable changes, such as make a web request for additional data based on the new value of your observable. Observables provide a `subscribe` function that lets you register a function to be called when the observable is updated.

Subscriptions use the same internal mechanism in Knockout that binding handlers and computed observables use to receive changes.

This is an example of setting up a subscription on an observable:

```
var locationId = ko.observable();
locationId.subscribe(function (newLocationId) {
  webService.getLocationDetails(newLocationId);
});
```

This subscription will be called any time when the `locationId` is updated, whether it happens from a UI binding or from somewhere else in JavaScript.

The `subscribe` function also allows you to provide a target for the subscription and the name of the event you want to subscribe to. The target is the value of `this` for the subscription handler you provide. The event defaults to change, which receives the value after it has been updated, but can also be `beforeChange`, which is called with the old value before a change happens:

```
locationId.subscribe(function (oldValue) {
  console.log("the location " + oldValue + " is about to change");
}, self, 'beforeChange');});
```

Finally, you can stop a subscription from continuing to fire by capturing it and calling dispose. This can be useful if you want to stop the handler or to make subscriptions that only fire a single time:

```
var subscription = locationId.subscribe(function (newValue) {
  console.log("the location " + oldValue + " is about to change");
  subscription.dispose();
});
```

Once a subscription has been disposed, it cannot be restarted. If you need it, you will have to recreate the subscription.

The `cp1-subscribe` branch has a subscription example that logs any changes to the `subtotal` observable on the JavaScript console, as well as a button that stops the subscription. Try changing the subtotal or total value and watch out for the console messages. Changing the total causes an update of the subtotal, which is why it still fires the subscription. Remember, changes from any source will cause an observable to report changes to all of its subscribers. This is the same reason updating the `total` computed causes the `subtotal` observable's input element to update; the input element is a subscriber to the viewmodel's property.

# Defining viewmodels

Viewmodels are the objects whose properties your view binds with; they form the binding context. It is the representation of your data and operations for your view (we will cover them in detail in the *Control flow bindings* section later in this chapter). Like regular objects in JavaScript, there are many ways to actually create them, but Knockout introduces some specific challenges.

# The this and self keywords

In JavaScript, `this` has a special meaning; it refers to the object calling the function. Functions called from an object get that object set to `this`. However, for functions that are anonymously called by code, that is merely the *inside* of an object, the behavior is different. Consider the following viewmodel:

```
function Invoice() {
  this.subtotal = ko.observable();
  this.total = ko.computed(function() {
  return this.subtotal() * 1.08; //Tax Rate
  });
}
```

The function inside the computed observable is not a property of the `Invoice` object. As it runs in a different context, its value for this will be the window object, not the `Invoice` object. It will not be able to find the `subtotal` property. There are two ways to handle this.

The first is by using the second parameter of the `ko.computed` function to bind the function to `this`:

```
function Invoice() {
  this.subtotal = ko.observable();
  this.total = ko.computed(function() {
    return this.subtotal() * 1.08; //Tax Rate
  }, this);
}
```

This gives the computed observable a reference to the `Invoice` that originally defined it, which allows the computed observable to call the supplied function in the correct context.

The second way to ensure the computed observable can reference the `subtotal`, is to capture the value of `this` in a closure. You can then use the closure to safely refer to the properties of the parent viewmodel. There are several conventional names for such a closure: `that`, `_this`, or `self`.

I prefer to use `self` as it is visually distinct from `this` while still carrying a similar meaning, but it's up to you:

```
function Invoice() {
  var self = this;
  self.subtotal = ko.observable();
  self.total = ko.computed(function() {
return self.subtotal() * 1.08; //Tax Rate
  });
}
```

I find the second method easier to remember. If you always use `self` to refer to the model, it will always work. If you have another anonymous function inside the computed, you will have to remember to bind that function as well; `self` continues to work as a closure no matter how many levels deep you nest. The `self` variable works as a closure inside any function defined in your viewmodel, including subscriptions. It's also easier to spot when `self` isn't being used, which is very helpful while debugging your code.

# Problems with prototypes

If you are working with viewmodels that will be inherited by other viewmodels, you might think that putting all the base observable properties on the prototype is the way to go. In vanilla JavaScript, if you are inheriting an object, try to change the value of a property stored on the prototype; the property would be added to the inheriting object leaving the prototype intact. When using observables in Knockout though, this isn't the case. The observables are functions, and their values are set by calling them with a single parameter, not by assigning new values to them. Because prototypical inheritance would result in multiple objects referring to a single observable; observables cannot be safely placed on viewmodel prototypes. Nonobservable functions can still be safely included in prototypes. For example, consider the following objects:

```
var protoVm = {
  name: ko.observable('New User')
};

var base1 = Object.create(protoVm);
var base2 = Object.create(protoVm);

base2.name("Base2");
```

The last line will cause the name of both objects to be updated, as it is referring to the same function. This example can be seen in the `cp1-prototype` branch, which includes two input elements bound to the name of each viewmodel. As they are really the same observable, changing one will affect the other.

# Serializing viewmodels

When you are ready to send your viewmodels to the server, or really do anything that requires you to work with their values instead of observables, Knockout provides two very handy utility methods:

- `ko.toJS`: This function takes an object and does a deep copy, unwrapping all observables, into a new JavaScript object whose properties are normal (nonobservable) JavaScript values. This function is perfect to get copies of viewmodels.
- `ko.toJSON`: This function uses the output from `ko.toJS` with `JSON.stringify` to produce a JSON string of the supplied object. This function accepts the same parameters as `JSON.stringify`.

# The data-bind syntax

Knockout takes advantage of the HTML5 `data-*` attribute specification to define its `data-bind` attribute. Though all HTML attributes are necessarily strings, Knockout parses them as name:value pairs. The name refers to the binding handler to be used and the value refers to the value the binding will use:

```
<button data-bind="enable: canSave">Save</button>
```

The `data-bind` attribute can also contain multiple bindings separated by commas. This allows multiple properties to be bound on an element:

```
<input data-bind="value: firstName, enable: canEdit" />
```

In the preceding example, the enable binding uses `canEdit` as a value. The binding will set the `disabled` attribute on the button element when `canEdit` is `false`, and remove the `disabled` attribute when `canEdit` is `true`. If `canEdit` is an observable, the enable binding will update whenever `canEdit` is updated. If `canEdit` is a literal value, such as `true`, it will only use the value to set the initial state.

Enable is a **one-way binding**; it will update the element with changes from the value but it will not update the value with changes from the element. This is because when enable is being used to control the element, Knockout assumes that nothing will be programmatically updating the element. Updates should happen in the viewmodel, and binding handlers should be responsible for ensuring the view is kept in sync.

When users update the UI of data-bound input elements, those changes need to be synced to the viewmodel. This is done with **two-way bindings**, such as the `value` binding:

```
<input data-bind="value: firstName" />
```

This binding will set the initial value of the `input` element to the current value of the `firstName` property, and after that, it will ensure that any changes to either the element's value or the property cause the other to update. If the user types something into the input, the `firstName` property will receive the value. If the `firstName` property is updated programmatically, the input's value will be updated.

These are both examples of binding against a simple property on the viewmodel. This is the most common case, but Knockout supports more complex scenarios as well.

 For a complete list of the standard Knockout binding handlers, see the Knockout documentation (`http://knockoutjs.com/documentation/introduction.html`).

# Binding with nested properties

In the previous example, Knockout parsed the binding value for the name of a property and looked for that property on the current viewmodel. You can also provide deep property references. Consider the following object:

```
var viewmodel = {
  user: {
    firstName: ko.observable('Tim'),
    age: ko.observable(27)
  }
};
```

We can bind directly against the `firstName` property of the viewmodel's user by using standard dot notation:

```
<input data-bind="value: user.firstName" />
```

# Binding against functions

If you are using the `click` or `event` bindings to bind some UI event, the binding expects the property to be a function. Functions will receive the current model (the binding context) as their first parameter, and the JavaScript event as the second parameter (though you shouldn't need to do this very often).

In this example, the parent viewmodel receives the contact to be removed from the `click` binding because the `foreach` loop creates a nested binding context for each contact. The parent reference in the binding moves the context up to the parent viewmodel to get access to the remove function:

```
<ul data-bind="foreach: contacts">
    <li>
      <span data-bind="text: name"></span>
      <button data-bind="click: $parent.remove">Remove</button>
    </li>
</ul>

var ViewModel = function() {
    var self = this;
    self.contacts = ko.observableArray([{ name: 'Tim' }, { name:
      'Bob' }]);
    self.remove = function (contact) {
        self.contacts.remove(contact);
    };
};
```

# Binding with expressions

In addition to property references, Knockout also supports the use of JavaScript expressions as binding values. For bindings that expect true or false values, such as enable, we can use Boolean expressions to set them:

```
<button data-bind="enable: age > 18">Approve</button>
```

We can also use ternary expressions to control the result of the expression. This is useful in cases where Booleans are not expected, such as text bindings:

```
Old enough to Drink in the U.S.
<span data-bind="text: age > 18 ? 'Yes' : 'No'"></span>
```

Now the `span` will have `Yes` as content.

Both forms of expressions will use dependency tracking to rerun if they read from an observable the first time they are run. If age was an observable value, we could update it and the element's binding would re-evaluate the expression, changing the text or enabled state if the result changed.

# Binding with function expressions

The last method to set binding values is by using functions. You can call a function by referencing it in the binding:

```
<button data-bind="enable: canApprove(age)">Approve</button>
```

You can also write an anonymous function as a string directly in the binding. When creating a function for the click binding, the parameters are the binding context (viewmodel) and the JavaScript click event. If you bind against a viewmodel function using its property name, it would receive the same parameters:

```
<button data-bind="text:
function(data) { console.log(data.age) }">Log Age</button>
```

Though this is possible, I wouldn't encourage it. It places logic directly in the view instead of in the viewmodel where it belongs. You should only use this last method in very special cases. It's much better to place the method on the viewmodel and just use a property reference.

# Using parentheses in bindings

It can be confusing trying to figure out when to use parentheses in bindings to use an observable as a value. Knockout tries to be helpful by not requiring the parentheses in simple binding expressions like this one:

```
<input data-bind="value: firstName" />
```

In this example, the firstName property could be either an observable or a literal value, and it would work just fine. However, there are two cases when the parentheses are needed in bindings: when binding against a nested property and when binding with an expression. Consider the following viewmodel:

```
var viewmodel = {
  user: ko.observable({
    firstName: ko.observable('Tim'),
    age: ko.observable(27)
  })
};
```

The user object here is an observable property, as are each of its properties. If we wanted to write the same binding now, it would need to include parentheses on the `user` function but still not on the `firstName` property:

```
<input data-bind="value: user().firstName" />
```

In cases where we are binding directly against a property, the parentheses of that property are never needed. This is because Knockout is smart enough to understand how to access the value of the observable that it is given in bindings.

However, if we are binding against an expression, they are always needed:

```
<button data-bind="enable: user().age > 18">Approve</button>
<button data-bind="enable: user().age() > 18">Approve</button>
```

Neither of these bindings will cause errors, but the first one will not work as expected. This is because the first expression will try to evaluate on the `age` observable itself (which is a function, not a number) instead of the observable's value. The second one correctly compares the value of the observable to `18`, producing the expected result.

## Debugging with ko.toJSON

Because `ko.toJSON` accepts the spaces argument for `JSON.stringify`, you can use it in a text binding to get a live copy of your viewmodel with nice, readable formatting:

```
<pre data-bind="text: ko.toJSON($root, null, 2)"></pre>
```

The `cp1-databind` branch has an interactive example of each of these bindings.

## Control flow bindings

So far, we have looked at one-way and two-way bindings that set or sync data with an attribute on an HTML element. There is a different kind of binding that Knockout uses for modifying the DOM by adding or removing nodes. These are the control flow bindings, and they include `foreach`, `if`, `with`, and `template`.

All of the control flow bindings work by actually removing their content from the DOM and creating an in-memory template from it. This template is used to add and remove the content as necessary.

Control flow bindings (except `if`) also introduce a binding context hierarchy. Your root binding context is the viewmodel passed to `ko.applyBindings`. The `data-bind` attributes have access to properties in the current context. Control flow bindings (other than `if`) create a child-binding context, meaning that `data-bind` attributes inside the control flow binding's template have access to the properties of their context and not the root context. Bindings inside a child context have access to special properties to allow them to navigate the context hierarchy. The most commonly used are:

- `$parent`: This accesses the binding context of the immediate parent. In this example, `group` and `$parent.group` refer to the same property because `$parent` accesses the context outside of the person:

```
<span data-bind="text: group"></span>
<div data-bind="with: person">
  <span data-bind="text: name"></span>
<span data-bind="text: $parent.group"></span>
  </div>
```

- `$parents[n]`: This is an array of parent contexts. The `$parents[0]` array is same as `$parent`.

- `$root`: This is the root viewmodel, the highest context in the hierarchy.

- `$data`: This is the current viewmodel, useful inside `foreach` loops.

 For a complete list of context properties, see the Knockout documentation for them at `http://knockoutjs.com/documentation/binding-context.html`.

# The if binding

The `if` binding takes a value or expression to evaluate and only renders the contained template when the value or expression is truthy (in the JavaScript sense). If the expression is falsy, the template is removed from the DOM. When the expression becomes true, the template is recreated and any contained `data-bind` attributes are reapplied. The `if` binding does not create a new binding context:

```
<div data-bind="if: isAdmin">
  <span data-bind="text: user.username"></span>
  <button data-bind="click: deleteUser">Delete</button>
</div>
```

This `div` would be empty when `isAdmin` is `false` or `null`. If the value of `isAdmin` is updated, the binding will re-evaluate and add or remove the template as necessary.

There is also an `ifnot` binding that just inverts the expression. It's useful if you want to still use a property reference without needing to add a bang and parentheses. The following two lines are equivalent:

```
<div data-bind="if: !isAdmin()" >
<div data-bind="ifnot: isAdmin">
```

The parentheses are needed in the first example because it is an expression, not a property name. They are not needed in the second example because it is a simple property reference.

# The with binding

The `with` binding creates a new binding context using the supplied value, which causes bindings inside the bound element to be scoped to the new context. These two snippets are functionally similar:

```
<div>
   First Name:
<span data-bind="text: selectedPerson().firstName"></span>
   Last Name:
<span data-bind="text: selectedPerson().lastName"></span>
</div>

<div data-bind="with: selectedPerson">
   First Name:
<span data-bind="text: firstName"></span>
   Last Name:
<span data-bind="text: lastName"></span>
</div>
```

While saving a few keystrokes and keeping your bindings easier to read is nice, the real benefit of the `with` binding is that it is an implicit `if` binding. If the value is `null` or `undefined`, the content of the HTML element will be removed from the DOM. In the cases where this is possible, it saves you from the need to make null checks for each descendant binding.

# The foreach binding

The `foreach` binding creates an implicit template using the contents of the HTML element and repeats that template for every element in the array.

This viewmodel contains a list of people we need to render:

```
var viewmodel = {
  people: [{name: 'Tim'}, {name: 'Justin}, {name: 'Mark'}]
}
```

With this binding, we create an implicit template for the `li` element:

```
<ul data-bind="foreach: people">
  <li data-bind="text: name"></li>
</ul>
```

This binding produces the following HTML:

```
<ul>
  <li>Tim</li>
  <li>Justin</li>
  <li>Mark</li>
</ul>
```

The thing to note here is that the `li` element is binding against `name`, which is the property of a person. Inside the `foreach` binding, the binding context is the child element. If you need to refer to the child itself, you can either use `$data` or supply an alias to the `foreach` binding.

The `$data` option is useful when the array only contains primitives that you want to bind against:

```
var viewmodel = {
  people: ['Tim', 'Justin, 'Mark']
}
...
<ul data-bind="foreach: people">
  <li data-bind="text: $data"></li>
</ul>
```

The `alias` option can clean up your code, but it is particularly useful when you have a nested context and want to refer to the parent. Refer to the following code:

```
<ul data-bind="foreach: { data: categories, as: 'category' }">
    <li>
        <ul data-bind="foreach: { data: items, as: 'item' }">
          <li>
            <span data-bind="text: category.name"></span>:
            <span data-bind="text: item"></span>
          </li>
        </ul>
    </li>
</ul>
```

This can be achieved with `$parent`, of course, but it is more legible when using an `alias`.

# Template binding

The template binding is a special control flow binding. It has a parameter for each of the other control flow bindings. It might be more accurate to say that the other control flow bindings are all **aliases** for the template binding:

```
<ul data-bind="foreach: { data: categories, as: 'category' }">
<ul data-bind="template: { foreach: categories, as: 'category' }">
```

Both of these are functionally equivalent. The template binding as has a parameter for `if` and `data` (which together make a `with` binding).

However, unlike the other control flow bindings, it can also generate its template from a named source using the `name` parameter. By default, the only source Knockout looks for is a `<script>` tag with an `id` parameter matching the `name` parameter:

```
<div data-bind="template: { name: 'person-template', data: seller
}"></div>
<script type="text/html" id="person-template">
    <h3 data-bind="text: name"></h3>
    <p>Credits: <span data-bind="text: credits"></span></p>
</script>
```

To stop the `script` block from being executed as JavaScript, you need a dummy script type, such as `text/html` or `text/ko`. Knockout will not apply bindings to script elements, but it will use them as a source for templates.

Though it is much more common to use the inline templates seen in `foreach` or `with`, named templates have three very important uses.

# Reusable templates

As templates can reference an external source for the HTML, it is possible to have multiple template bindings pointing to a single source:

```
<div>
  <div data-bind="template: { name: 'person', data: father} "></div>
  <div data-bind="template: { name: 'person', data: mother} "></div>
</div>
...
<script type="text/html" id="person">
  <h3 data-bind="text: name"></h3>
  <strong>Age: </strong>
<span data-bind="text: age"></span><br>
  <strong>Location: </strong>
<span data-bind="text: location"></span><br>
  <strong>Favorite Color: </strong>
<span data-bind="text: favoriteColor"></span><br>
</script>
```

The branch `cp1-reuse` has an example of this technique.

# Recursive templates

Because templates participate in data-binding themselves, it is possible for a template to bind against itself. If a template references itself, the result is recursive:

```
<div data-bind="template: { name: 'personTemplate', data: forefather}
"></div>

<script type="text/html" id="personTemplate">
  <h4 data-bind="text: name"></h4>
  <ul data-bind="foreach: children">
    <li data-bind="template: 'personTemplate'"></li>
  </ul>
</script>
```

The template reference in the preceding template is using the shorthand binding, which just takes the name of the template directly. When using this shorthand, the current binding context is used for the template's `data` parameter, which is perfect inside a `foreach` loop like this one. This is a common technique when using recursive templates, as trees of information are the most common place to find visual recursion.

An example of this recursive template is in the `cp1-recurse` branch.

# Dynamic templates

The name of the template in the previous example is a string, but it could be a property reference too. Binding the template name to an observable allows you to control which template is rendered. This could be useful to swap a viewmodel's template between a display and edit mode. Consider this template binding:

```
<div data-bind="template: { name: template, data: father} "></div>
```

This template binding backed by a viewmodel property such as this one:

```
self.template = ko.computed(function() {
    return self.editing() ? 'editTemplate' : 'viewTemplate';
});
```

If we update the editing property from true to false, the template will re-render from viewTemplate to editTemplate. This allows us to programmatically switch between them.

An example of a dynamic edit/view template is in the cp1-dynamic branch.

In an advanced scenario, you could use a technique such as this for creating a generic container on a page to display entirely different views. Switching the template name and the data at the same time would mimic navigation, creating a **Single Page Application (SPA)**. We will take a look at a similar technique when we get to *Chapter 4, Application Development with Components and Modules.*

# Containerless control flow

So far, we have looked at using the control flow bindings (if, with, foreach, and template) and the standard data-bind attribute on an HTML element. It is also possible to use control flow bindings without an element by using special comment tags that are parsed by Knockout. This is called containerless control flow.

Adding a <!— ko --> comment starts a virtual element that ends with a <!-- /ko --> comment. This virtual element causes a control flow binding to treat all contained elements as children. The following block of code demonstrates how sibling elements can be grouped by a virtual comment container:

```
<ul>
    <li>People</li>
    <li>Locations</li>
    <!-- ko if: isAdmin -->
    <li>Users</li>
    <li>Admin</li>
    <!-- /ko -->
</ul>
```

List elements only allow specific elements as children. The preceding containerless syntax applies the `if` binding to the last two elements in the list, which causes them to add or remove from the DOM based in the `isAdmin` property:

```
<ul>
    <li>Nav Header</li>
    <!-- ko foreach: navigationItems -->
    <li><span data-bind="text: $data"></span></li>
    <!-- /ko -->
</ul>
```

The preceding containerless syntax allows us to have a `foreach` binding to create a list of items while maintaining a header item at the top of the list.

All of the control flow bindings can be used in this way. The preceding two examples can be seen in the `cp1-containerless` branch.

# Extenders

The last "basic" feature to cover is extenders (don't worry, there is still plenty of advanced stuff to cover). Extenders offer a way to modify individual observables. Two common uses of extenders are as follows:

- Adding properties or functions to the observable
- Adding a wrapper around the observable to modify writes or reads

## Simple extenders

Adding an extender is as simple as adding a new function to the `ko.extenders` object with the name you want to use. This function receives the observable being extended (called the target) as the first argument, and any configuration passed to the extender is received as the second argument, as shown in the following code:

```
ko.extenders.recordChanges = function(target, options) {
  target.previousValues = ko.observableArray();
  target.subscribe(function(oldValue) {
    target.previousValues.push(oldValue);
  }, null, 'beforeChange');
  return target;
};
```

This extender will create a new `previousValues` property on the observable. This new property is as an observable array and old values are pushed to it as the original observable is changed (the current value is already in the observable of course).

The reason the extender has to return the target is because the result of the extender is the new observable. The need for this is apparent when looking at how the extender is called:

```
var amount = ko.observable(0).extend({ recordChanges: true});
```

The `true` value sent to `recordChanges` is received by the extender as the `options` parameter. This value can be any JavaScript value, including objects and functions.

You can also add multiple extenders to an observable in the same call. The object sent to the `extend` method will call an observable for every property it contains:

```
var amount = ko.observable(0).extend({ recordChanges: true,
    anotherExtender: { intOption: 1});
```

As the `extend` method is called on the observable, usually during its initial creation, the result of the `extend` call is what is actually stored. If the target is not returned, the `amount` variable would not be the intended observable.

To access the extended value, you would use `amount.previousValues()` from JavaScript, or `amount.previousValues` if accessing it from a binding. Note the lack of parentheses after amount; because `previousValues` is a property of the observable, not a property of the observable's value, it is accessed directly. This might not be immediately obvious, but it should make sense as long as you remember that the observable and the value the observable contains are two different JavaScript objects.

An example of this extender is in the `cp1-extend` branch.

# Extenders with options

The previous example does not pass any options to the `recordChanges` extender, it just uses `true` because the property requires a value to be a valid JavaScript. If you want a configuration for your extender, you can pass it as this value, and a complex configuration can be achieved by using another object as the value.

If we wanted to supply a list of values that are not to be recorded, we could modify the extender to use the options as an array:

```
ko.extenders.recordChanges = function(target, options) {
  target.previousValues = ko.observableArray();
  target.subscribe(function(oldValue) {
    if (!(options.ignore && options.ignore.indexOf(oldValue) !== -
      1))
      target.previousValues.push(oldValue)
```

```
    }, null, 'beforeChange');
    return target;
};
```

Then we could call the extender with an array:

```
var history = ko.observable(0).extend({
  recordChanges: { ignore: [0, null] }
});
```

Now our `history` observable won't record values for `0` or `null`.

# Extenders that replace the target

Another common use for extenders is to wrap the observable with a computed observable that modifies reads or writes, in which case, it would return the new observable instead of the original target.

Let's take our `recordChanges` extender a step further and actually block writes that are in our `ignore` array (never mind that an extender named `recordChanges` should never do something like this in the real world!):

```
ko.extenders.recordChanges = function(target, options) {
  var ignore = options.ignore instanceof Array ? options.ignore : [];
  //Make sure this value is available
  var result = ko.computed({
    read: target,
    write: function(newValue) {
      if (ignore.indexOf(newValue) === -1) {
        result.previousValues.push(target());
        target(newValue);
      } else {
        target.notifySubscribers(target());
      }
    }
  }).extend({ notify: 'always'});

  result.previousValues = ko.observableArray();

  //Return the computed observable
  return result;
};
```

That's a lot of changes, so let's unpack them.

First, to make ignore easier to reference, I've set a new variable that will either be the options.ignore property or an empty array. Defaulting to an empty array lets us skip the null check later, which makes the code a little easier to read. Second, I created a writable computed observable. The read function just routes to the target observable, but the write function will only write to the target if the ignore option doesn't contain the new value. Otherwise, it will notify the target subscribers of the old value. This is necessary because if a UI binding on the observable initiated the change, it needs the illegal change to be reverted. The UI element would already have updated and the easiest way to change it back is through the standard binding notification mechanism that is already listening for changes.

The last change is the notify: always extender that's on the result. This is one of Knockout's default extenders. Normally, an observable will only report changes to subscribers when the value has been modified. To get the observable to reject changes, it needs to be able to notify subscribers of its current unchanged value. The notify extender forces the observable to always report changes, even when they are the same.

Finally, the extender returns the new computed observable instead of the target, so that anyone trying to write a value does so against the computed.

The cp1-extendreplace branch has an example of this binding. Notice that trying to enter values into the input box that are included in the ignored options (0 or an empty string) are immediately reverted.

# The Contacts List application

It's time to start putting these concepts together into a usable application. Isolated samples can only take you so far. We are going to cover the application in the cp1-contacts branch in detail. The application's functionality is all on the **Contacts** page, which you can get to from the navigation bar in your browser. Before we start digging into the code, I encourage you to play around with the application a bit (it does persist data). It will help in understanding the relationships in the code.

# Overview

The application has three main JavaScript objects:

- The contact model
- The **Contacts** page viewmodel
- The mock data service

The application only uses the HTML in the `index.html` file, but the two sections are mostly independent.

- The entry form (create and edit)
- The contacts list

The JavaScript code in the example follows the **Immediately-Invoked Function Expression (IIFE)** pattern (sometimes pronounced "iffy") to isolate code from the global scope, and a namespace called `app` to share code between files:

```
(function(app, $, ko) {
  /* CODE IN HERE */
})(window.app = window.app || {}, jQuery, ko);
```

This is definitely not the only way to organize JavaScript code, and you may have a pattern you prefer. If you want to understand this pattern better, here are a few online resources:

- `http://benalman.com/news/2010/11/immediately-invoked-function-expression/`
- `http://addyosmani.com/blog/essential-js-namespacing/`

# The contact model

The `client/app/contacts.js` file defines our basic contact object. Let's go over it piece by piece.

It starts with a standard declaration of observable properties with some default values. There are a lot of reasons to organize code in a variety of ways, but for the smaller models, I prefer to keep all of their persistable properties together at the top:

```
app.Contact = function(init) {
  var self = this;
  self.id = ko.observable(0);
  self.firstName = ko.observable('');
  self.lastName = ko.observable('');
  self.nickname = ko.observable('');
  self.phoneNumber = ko.observable('');
  /* More below */
```

Next is the `displayName` property, some simple logic to generate a nice "title" for UI display. The JavaScript or operator (||) is used here to ensure we don't try to read the `length` property on a `null` or `undefined` value by returning a default value in case all the names are empty. This essentially makes it a null-coalescing operator when used during an assignment:

```
self.displayName = ko.computed(function() {
    var nickname = self.nickname() || '';
    if (nickname.length > 0)
      return nickname;
    else if ((self.firstName() || '').length > 0)
      return self.firstName() + ' ' + self.lastName();
    else
      return 'New Contact';
});
```

Next is a utility method to update the model that accepts an object and merges in its properties. I generally put a similar method onto all of my models so that I have a standard way of updating them. Once again, we are using || as a safety net, in case the method is called without a parameter (in the real world, you would want a stronger check, one that ensured `update` was an object and not a primitive value or an array):

```
//Generic update method, merge all properties into the viewmodel
self.update = function(update) {
  data = update || {};
  Object.keys(data).forEach(function(prop) {
    if (ko.isObservable(self[prop]))
      self[prop](data[prop]);
  });
};

//Set the initial values using our handy-dandy update method.
self.update(init);
```

Also note that after defining the `update` function, the model calls it with the constructor argument. This lets the constructor provide the ability to create a new model from existing data and partial data as well. This is very useful when deserializing data, for example, JSON from an Ajax request.

Lastly, we have the `toJSON` method. The standard `JSON.stringify` method in JavaScript will look for this method to allow an object to control how it is serialized. As Knockout's `ko.toJSON` calls `JSON.stringify` underneath after it unwraps all the observables so that the serialization gets values and not functions.

As the serialized form of our model is the one we will try to persist, usually by sending it to the server with Ajax, we don't want to include things such as our computed display name. Our `toJSON` method override takes care of this by just deleting the property:

```
//Remove unwanted properties from serialized data
    self.toJSON = function() {
      var copy = ko.toJS(self);
      delete copy.displayName;
      return copy;
    };
```

The copy with `ko.toJS` is important. We don't want to delete `displayName` from the actual model; we only want it removed from the serialized model. If we made the variable with `copy = self`, we would just have a reference to the same object. The `ko.toJS` method is a simple way to get a plain JavaScript copy that we can safely delete properties from without affecting the original object.

# The Contacts page viewmodel

The `client/app/contactspage.js` file defines the viewmodel for the **Contacts** page. Unlike our contacts model, the page does a lot more than expose some observable properties, and it isn't designed to be constructed from existing data either. Instead of taking an object to control its starting values, which doesn't make much sense for a page, the constructor's argument is designed for dependency injection; its constructor arguments take in its external dependencies.

In this example, `dataService` is a dependency used by the page viewmodel:

```
app.ContactsPageViewmodel = function(dataService)
```

Very briefly, if you aren't familiar with dependency injection, it lets us define our page against an API (sometimes called a contract or interface) of methods to get and save data. This is especially useful for us, as in this sample application, we aren't using real Ajax but mocking it with an object that just writes to the DOM's local storage:

```
ko.applyBindings
  (new app.ContactsPageViewmodel(app.mockDataService));
```

 For more information on the DOM local storage, see the page on the Mozilla Developer Network at `https://developer.mozilla.org/en-US/docs/Web/Guide/API/DOM/Storage`.

However, when we write the real Ajax service later, our `ContactsPageViewmodel` doesn't need to change at all. We will just construct it with a different `dataService` parameter. As long as they expose the same methods (the same API) it will just work.

The first section inside the constructor is for the contacts list. We expose an observable array and get the contacts from our data service:

```
self.contacts = ko.observableArray();

dataService.getContacts(function(contacts) {
  self.contacts(contacts);
});
```

We are passing callback to the `getContacts` call because our data service provides an asynchronous API. When the data service has finished getting our contacts, it will call the callback with them. All our callback needs to do is put them into the `contacts` array.

The next block of code is to control the **CRUD (Create, Read, Update, Delete)** operations for individual contacts. First, we expose an observable object that we will use for all edits:

```
self.entryContact = ko.observable(null);

    self.newEntry = function() {
      self.entryContact(new app.Contact());
    };
    self.cancelEntry = function() {
      self.entryContact(null);
    };
```

Our UI is going to bind an edit form against the `entryContact` property. The entry contact property is pulling a double duty here; it contains the contact that is being created or edited, and it indicates that editing is occurring. If the entry contact is null, then we aren't editing; if it has an object, then we are editing. The UI will use `with` and `if` bindings to control which content to show based on this logic.

The `newEntry` and `cancelEntry` functions provide the UI with a means to switch between these two states.

For editing existing contacts, we just expose another function that takes a contact and sets the entry contact to it:

```
self.editContact = function(contact) {
     self.entryContact(contact);
   };
```

The last thing we need for real editing is the ability to persist our changes. As in the real world, we have three scenarios, namely creating new objects, saving existing objects, and deleting existing objects.

Creating and updating are both going to be done using the `entryContact` property, and we want to be able to bind the same form for both, which means we need to target a single function:

```
self.saveEntry = function() {
  if (self.entryContact().id() === 0) {
    dataService.createContact(self.entryContact(), function() {
      self.contacts.push(self.entryContact());
      self.entryContact(null);
    });
  } else {
    dataService.updateContact(self.entryContact(), function() {
      self.entryContact(null);
    });
  }
};
```

Internally, our `saveEntry` method checks for a non-default `id` value to determine whether or not it's making a new object or updating an existing one. Both are calls to the data service using the entry contact with a callback to clear the `entryContact` property out (as we are done with editing). In the creation case, we also want to add the newly created contact to our local list of contacts before emptying the entry contact:

```
self.contacts.push(self.entryContact());
self.entryContact(null);
```

You might think that the contact is going to be null out by the second line, but that is not the case. The `entryContact` property is an observable and its value is a contact. The first line reads this value and pushes it into the `contacts` array. The second line sets the value of the `entryContact` property to `null`; it does not affect the contact that was just pushed. It's the same as if we had set a variable to null after adding it to an array. The variable was a reference to the object, and making the variable null removes the reference, not the object itself.

The delete function is simple by comparison:

```
self.deleteContact = function(contact) {
    dataService.removeContact(contact.id(), function() {
      self.contacts.remove(contact);
    });
  };
```

It's going to take an existing contact, like `editContact` did, and call the data service. As we are deleting the contact, the only thing we need is the `id` property. The callback will remove the contact from the list of contacts when the service is done, using the `remove` function provided on all observable arrays by Knockout.

The last piece of functionality on the page is the search mechanism. It starts with an observable to track the search and a function to clear it out:

```
self.query = ko.observable('');
self.clearQuery = function() { self.query(''); };
```

The `query` property is going to be used to filter out any contacts that don't have a matching or partially-matching property. If we wanted to be as flexible as possible, we could search against every property. However, since our list of contacts is only going to show our computed `displayName` and phone number, it would look odd to return results matching on properties we didn't show. This is the computed observable from the code sample that filters the contacts list:

```
self.displayContacts = ko.computed(function() {
  //No query, just return everything
  if (self.query() === '')
    return self.contacts();
  var query = self.query().toLowerCase();
  //Otherwise, filter all contacts using the query
  return ko.utils.arrayFilter(self.contacts(), function(c) {
    return c.displayName().toLowerCase().indexOf(query) !== -1
        || c.phoneNumber().toLowerCase().indexOf(query) !== -1;
  });
});
```

 If you want to filter all of the contact's properties, they are listed in the repository code as comments. They can easily be re-enabled by uncommenting each line.

First, we check to see whether the query is empty, because if it is, we aren't going to filter anything so we don't want to waste cycles iterating the contacts anyway.

Before starting, we call the `toLowerCase()` function on the query to avoid any case sensitivity issues. Then, we iterate on the contacts. Knockout provides several utilities methods for arrays (among other things) on the `ko.utils` object. The `arrayFilter` function takes an array and an iterator function, which is called on each element of the array. If the function returns `true`, `arrayFilter` will include that element in its return value; otherwise it will filter the element out. All our iterator needs to do is compare the properties we want to keep the filter on (remembering to put them in lowercase first).

Now if the UI binds against `displayContacts`, the search functionality will filter the UI.

However, we might experience poor performance with a large list of contacts if we are looping through them all every time the query is updated, especially if the query updates every time a key is pressed. To address this, we can use the standard Knockout `rateLimit` extender on our filtered computed to stop it from updating too frequently:

```
self.displayContacts = ko.computed(function() {
  /* computed body */
}).extend({
  rateLimit: {
    timeout: 100,
    method: 'notifyWhenChangesStop'
  }
});
```

This extender has two modes: `notifyAtFixedRate` and `notifyWhenChangesStop`. These two options will throttle or debounce the computed.

 If you aren't familiar with the throttling and debouncing functions, there is an excellent explanation with visuals at `http://drupalmotion.com/article/debounce-and-throttle-visual-explanation`.

This lets us control how often the computed re-evaluates itself. The preceding example will only re-evaluate the computed once all dependencies have stopped changing for 100 ms. This will let the UI update when the query typing settles down while still appearing to filter as the user types.

# A philosophical note on a model versus a viewmodel

The line between model and viewmodel in client-server application can get blurry, and even after reading Knockout's documentation (`http://knockoutjs.com/documentation/observables.html`) it can be unclear whether or not our contact object is really a model or viewmodel. Most would probably argue that it is a viewmodel as it has observables. I like to think of these smaller objects, which are barely more than their persisted data, as models and to think of viewmodels as the objects containing operations and view representations, such as our **Contacts** page viewmodel `removeContact` operation or the `entryContact` property.

# Mock data service

Normally, you would use an Ajax call, probably with jQuery, to retrieve data and submit data to and from the server. Because this is a book on Knockout and not Node.js, I wanted to keep the server as thin as possible. From the "Mastering Knockout" perspective, whether we call a JavaScript object making Ajax requests or store it in the DOM is immaterial. As long as we are working with something that looks and functions like an asynchronous service, we can explore how Knockout viewmodels might interact with it. That being said, there is some functionality in the data service that would be used in an Ajax data service object, and it is interesting from a Knockout application development perspective.

You might have noticed in the previous section that when the **Contacts** page view model communicated with the data service, it wasn't dealing with JSON but real JavaScript objects. In fact, not even plain JavaScript objects but our contact model. This is because part of the data service's responsibility, whether it's a mock or a real Ajax service, is to abstract away the knowledge of the service mechanisms. In our case, this means translating between JSON and our Knockout models:

```
createContact: function(contact, callback) {
  $.ajax({
      type: "POST",
      url: "/contacts",
      data: ko.toJS(contact)
    })
    .done(function(response) {
      contact.id(response.id);
      callback()
    });
}
```

This is the `createContact` method from our mock data service if it was rewritten to use real Ajax (this code is in the `mockDataService.js` file as a comment). The data service is part of our application, so it knows that it's working with observable properties and that it needs to translate them into plain JavaScript for jQuery to properly serialize it, so it unwraps the contact that it's given with `ko.toJS`. Then, in the `done` handler, it takes the `id` that it gets back from the server's response and updates the contact's observable `id` property with it. Finally, it calls the callback to signify that it's done.

You might wonder why it doesn't pass `contact` as an argument to the callback. It certainly could, but it isn't necessary. The original caller already had the contact, and the only thing that the caller is going to need is the new `id` value. We've already updated the `id`, and as it's observable, any subscriber will pick that new value up. If we needed some special handling before setting the `id` value, that would be a different case and we could raise the callback with `id` as an argument.

# The view

Hopefully, you have already played with the application a bit. If you haven't, now is the time. I'll wait.

You would have noticed that when adding or editing contacts, the contacts list is removed. What you might not have noticed is that the URL doesn't change; the browser isn't actually navigating when we switch between these two views. Though they are in the same HTML file, these two different views are mostly independent and they are controlled through a `with` and an `ifnot` binding.

# The edit form

This is what is shown when adding or editing contacts:

```
<form class="form" role="form" data-bind="with: entryContact,
  submit: saveEntry">
    <h2 data-bind="text: displayName"></h2>
    <div class="form-group">
      <label for="firstName" class="control-label">First Name
        </label>
      <input type="text" class="form-control" id="firstName"
        placeholder="First Name" data-bind="value: firstName">
    </div>
    <div class="form-group">
      <label for="lastName" class="control-label">Last Name
        </label>
      <input type="text" class="form-control" id="lastName"
        placeholder="First Name" data-bind="value: lastName">
    </div>
    <div class="form-group">
      <label for="nickname" class="control-label">Nickname
        </label>
      <input type="text" class="form-control" id="nickname"
        placeholder="First Name" data-bind="value: nickname">
    </div>
    <div class="form-group">
```

```
          <label for="phoneNumber" class="control-label">
            Phone Number</label>
          <input type="tel" class="form-control" id="phoneNumber"
            placeholder="First Name" data-bind="value: phoneNumber">
        </div>
        <div class="form-group">
          <button type="submit" class="btn btn-primary">Save
            </button>
          <button data-bind="click: $parent.cancelEntry"
            class="btn btn-danger">Cancel</button>
        </div>
      </form>
```

Because the `with` binding is also implicitly an `if` binding, the entire form is hidden when the `entryContact` property is null or undefined.

The rest of the form is pretty straightforward. A `submit` binding is used so that clicking the save button or hitting the enter key on any field calls the submit handler, a header showing the display name, value bindings for each field, a save button with `type="submit"` (so that it uses the submit handler), and a cancel button that binds to `$parent.cancelEntry`. Remember, the `$parent` scope is necessary because the `with` binding creates a binding context on the `entry` contact and `cancelEntry` is a function on `ContactPageViewmodel`.

# Contacts list

The list starts with an `ifnot` binding on the `entryContact` property, ensuring that it only shows in the case that the previous form is hidden. We only want one or the other to be seen at a time:

```
<div data-bind="ifnot: entryContact">
  <h2>Contacts</h2>
  <div class="row">
    <div class="col-xs-8">
      <input type="search" class="form-control"
        data-bind="value: query, valueUpdate: 'afterkeydown'"
          placeholder="Search Contacts">
    </div>
    <div class="col-xs-4">
      <button class="btn btn-primary" data-bind="click: newEntry">
        Add Contact</button>
    </div>
  </div>
  <ul class="list-unstyled" data-bind="foreach: displayContacts">
    <li>
```

```
<h3>
  <span data-bind="text: displayName"></span>
    <small data-bind="text: phoneNumber"></small>
  <button class="btn btn-sm btn-default"
    data-bind="click: $parent.editContact">Edit</button>
  <button class="btn btn-sm btn-danger"
    data-bind="click: $parent.deleteContact">Delete</button>
</h3>
      </li>
    </ul>
  </div>
```

The search input has a `value` binding as well as the `valueUpdate` option. The value update option controls when the `value` binding reports changes. By default, changes are reported on blur, but the `afterkeydown` setting causes changes to be reported immediately after the input gets a new letter. This would cause the search to update in real time, but remember that the display contacts have a `rateLimit` extender that debounces the updates to 100 ms.

Next to the search box is a button to add a new contact. Then, of course, the list of contacts is bound with a `foreach` binding on the `displayContacts` property. If it was bound against `contacts` directly, the list would not show the filtering. Depending on your application, you might even want to keep the unfiltered contacts list private and only expose the filtered lists. The best option really does depend on what else you're doing, and in most cases, it's okay to use your personal preference.

Inside the contacts list, each item shows the display name for the phone number, with a button to edit or delete the contact. As `foreach` creates a binding context on the individual contact and the edit and delete functions are on the parent, the `click` binding uses the `$parent` context property. The `click` binding also sends the current model to each of the edit and delete functions, so that these functions don't have to try to find the right JavaScript object by looking through the full list.

That's really all there is to the application. We've got a list view with searching that switches to a view that's reused easily for both editing and creating.

# Summary

In most of this chapter, we reviewed the use of standard Knockout. Hopefully, I didn't lose you in the weeds back there. The important thing is that before we move on to extending Knockout with custom functionality or building larger applications, you must feel comfortable with the basic use of observables and data binding. This includes:

- **Defining viewmodels**: This includes creating observables, binding functions, and handling serialization
- **Writing bindings**: This includes using properties, expressions, inline functions, and when to use parentheses
- **Extenders**: This includes creating extenders and extending observables
- **Templates**: This tells us how the flow of control works, what a binding context is, inline versus named templates, and containerless control flow

In the next chapter, we will be adding new functionalities to Knockout by creating our own binding handlers.

# 2
# Extending Knockout with Custom Binding Handlers

Knockout's standard bindings are great. They solve most of the general problems you are likely to encounter when developing web apps. But there is always the need to provide something special, whether you are working on your own library or just trying to add a bit of style to your app. When that happens, you will want to provide that functionality through the same binding system you are using everywhere else. Luckily, Knockout makes extending this system easy. In this chapter, we will be looking at how to make our own binding handlers. We will be covering the following topics:

- What a binding handler contains
- Creating new binding handlers
- Using custom binding handlers to integrate with third-party libraries
- Managing binding contexts
- Using the containerless control flow syntax with custom bindings

Creating custom binding handlers for new and more complex HTML interactions is a key to developing feature-rich applications. While the basics are easy to learn, there are enough extension points to support just about any use case. We are going to be looking at plenty of examples to get a solid idea of what binding handlers are capable of and how we can make the best use of them.

## The data binding pattern

This section is primarily philosophical. If you feel like you already have a solid understanding of the *what* and *why* behind the **Model-View-ViewModel (MVVM)** pattern and binding handlers, then you might want to skip to the next section, *Components of a binding handler*.

Okay, let's talk about patterns and practices. If you haven't worked with WPF before, then the MVVM pattern is probably the most confusing thing about Knockout. MVVM is a pattern that came out of Microsoft. It doesn't get a lot of attention outside the .NET community, and it's similar enough to the far more popular MVC pattern because of which confusion is nearly guaranteed.

In MVVM, the viewmodel is supposed to represent an abstraction of the view. Consider these two lists of message threads in iOS:

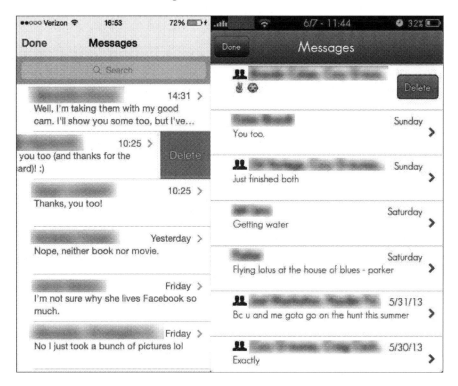

They both show a list of threads, and each thread contains a title showing the person it is with, an excerpt from the most recent message, and a timestamp. A thread can be selected or deleted. To select a message, you can touch it. To delete a message, you can slide left to bring up the **Delete** button, and then press the **Delete** button to delete the thread. You might be able to spot a difference in behavior already though. The list on the left slides the entire thread left to reveal the **Delete** button, pushing the thread partially off the screen. The list on the right superimposes the button on top of the thread, hiding the timestamp.

These differences are entirely part of the presentation of the data. Both of these views could, and should, be supported by the same viewmodel. They are both showing the same data and allow the same actions.

To be able to consume this data using the intended behavior (slide-reveal or slide-superimpose), the view needs support from something besides the viewmodel. In the MVVM pattern, this is the domain of the binding handler, and even though the binding handler doesn't get a letter in the acronym, it's still a critical piece of the puzzle. As the viewmodel is not supposed to know about view-related concepts such as buttons, clicks, or finger-taps, and the view is supposed to be entirely declarative; a binding handler is required to glue the two together.

The underlying principle here is the separation of concerns. The view is concerned with UI elements and interactions. The viewmodel is concerned with code objects and actions, and binding handlers are concerned with generically translating between specific UI elements or actions to and from the viewmodel.

As that's out of the way, time to get started with creating some custom binding handlers!

# Components of a binding handler

Binding handlers are defined by adding objects to the `ko.bindingHandlers` object, just like extenders. They are composed of an `init` and an `update` function.

The `init` function runs when the binding is first applied to the element either when `ko.applyBindings` is called or when the element is created by a control flow binding, such as `template` or `foreach`. It should be used for all one-time work such as attaching event handlers or disposal callbacks to the element.

The `update` function runs just after `init` does, when the binding is first applied. It runs again anytime when any observable dependencies are changed. The `update` function determines its dependencies just like a computed observable does. If an observable is accessed when an update runs, it subscribes to that observable. The `update` function should be used to keep the UI in sync with changes from the viewmodel:

```
ko.bindingHandlers.yourBindingName = {
    init: function(element, valueAccessor, allBindings, viewModel,
      bindingContext) {
        // This will be called when the binding is first applied
        // Set up any initial state, event handlers, etc. here
    },
    update: function(element, valueAccessor, allBindings,
      viewModel, bindingContext) {
        // This will be called once when the binding is first applied
        // and again whenever dependant observables change.
        // Update the DOM element based on the supplied values here.
    }
};
```

Both functions receive the following parameters:

- `Element`: This is the DOM element the binding was applied to.

- `valueAccessor`: This is a function that will return the result of the binding expression. For example, if the binding was `value: name`, then `valueAccessor` would return the `name` property. If `name` was an observable, you would still need to either call it or pass it to `ko.unwrap` (this function will be covered in the next section) to get the value. If the binding was `value: name() + '!'`, then `valueAccessor` would return the resulting string.

- `allBindings`: This is an object with a `get` and `has` function for accessing other bindings on the element.

- `Viewmodel`: In previous versions of Knockout, this gave access to the viewmodel, but it has been deprecated in favor of `bindingContext.$data` or `bindingContext.$rawData` as of Knockout 3.0.

- `bindingContext`: This is an object with the current binding context for the binding. This has the special binding context properties such as `$parent` and `$root`. This parameter was introduced in Knockout 3.0.

# Using custom binding handlers

Once added to the `ko.bindingHandler` object, custom bindings are no different from normal bindings. If you add a binding handler named `flash`, you could use it on an HTML element with a standard `data-bind` attribute:

```
<p data-bind="flash: vmProperty">Flashy! (bum dum tish)</p>
```

# Simple binding handlers

Binding handlers can range from very simple to whole applications by themselves. As the purpose of binding handlers is to translate between the presentation layer (HTML) and the viewmodel (JavaScript), the binding handler's complexity is directly related to the complexity of the UI interaction and the bound data. Simple tasks such as hiding or showing an element with animation will have very thin handlers, while data binding on an interactive map element will require much more logic.

# Animated binding handlers

As DOM interaction in the primary use case for jQuery, and given its popularity, it is not uncommon to use jQuery inside Knockout binding handlers. The canonical custom binding handler example from the Knockout documentation is a binding to hide and show elements, with the jQuery's `slideUp` and `slideDown` methods, instead of using the standard `visible` binding to switch them on and off:

```
ko.bindingHandlers.slideVisible = {
    init: function(element, valueAccessor) {
        var value = ko.unwrap(valueAccessor());
        $(element).toggle(value);
    },
    update: function(element, valueAccessor, allBindings) {
        var value = ko.unwrap(valueAccessor());
        var duration = allBindings.get('slideDuration') || 400;

        if (value === true)
            $(element).slideDown(duration); //show
        else
            $(element).slideUp(duration); //hide
    }
};
```

This example uses both an `init` and `update` function. The `init` function here is necessary to ensure that a value starting out as false doesn't cause the element to slide up when bindings are first applied, or vice versa. Without it, the `update` function would run right away and try to hide the element by sliding it up. The `init` function ensures that the element is already in the correct visible state, so that an animation doesn't occur when the binding first runs.

`ko.unwrap` is a utility method that will return the value of an observable if called with one; otherwise it will just return the first argument directly. It's perfect if you don't know whether you have an observable or not as it's safe to call it with anything. Most custom bindings should be able to support observable and nonobservable values, so you should always unwrap the `valueAccessor` parameter, unless you have a good reason not to.

The check for `allBindings.get('slideDuration')` allows a configurable value to be used for the slide timing. The `allBinding` object gives us access to other bindings that were used on the same element and is commonly used to collect optional configuration values:

```
<p data-bind="slideVisible: isShowing, slideDuration:
    200">Quick</p>
```

This lets the view determine how fast or slow to hide and show the element. As the animation speed is a part of the presentation, it makes sense for it to be configured from the view. If you want to use a viewmodel observable for slideDuration, you can modify that line to unwrap the value:

```
var duration = ko.unwrap(allBindings.get('slideDuration')) || 400;
```

An example of this binding is in the cp2-slide branch.

# Working with third-party controls

The slideVisible binding is a perfectly simple binding; it has a basic init function to start the binding and has an update function that modifies the DOM when the viewmodel changes. It is a **one way binding** though, only watching the viewmodel for changes. **Two way bindings** also need to watch the DOM element for changes and send it back to the viewmodel. Generally, this is accomplished by attaching an event handler in the init function; remember that the update function runs every time dependencies change, so attaching an event handler there would result in the event handler being attached multiple times.

Binding handlers can also be used to integrate with third-party controls. Though HTML5 has a native datepicker control, you might need one that is more backwards-compatible. The datepicker control of jQuery is a nice out-of-the-box control, but it requires a call to $(element).datepicker() to convert a standard input element. A binding handler is the perfect place to run this initialization logic for the view:

```
ko.bindingHandlers.datepicker = {
    init: function(element, valueAccessor, allBindingsAccessor) {
        var options = allBindingsAccessor().datepickerOptions || {},
            $el = $(element);

        //initialize datepicker with some optional options
        $el.datepicker(options);

        //handle the field changing
        ko.utils.registerEventHandler(element, "change",
          function() {
            var observable = valueAccessor();
            observable($el.datepicker("getDate"));
        });

        //handle disposal (if KO removes by the template binding)
        ko.utils.domNodeDisposal.addDisposeCallback
          (element, function() {
```

```
                    $el.datepicker("destroy");
            });

    },
    update: function(element, valueAccessor) {
        var value = ko.unwrap(valueAccessor()),
            $el = $(element),
            current = $el.datepicker("getDate");

        if (value - current !== 0) {
            $el.datepicker("setDate", value);
        }
    }
};
```

To use this binding in HTML, apply it to an input element:

```
<input data-bind="datepicker: myDate, datepickerOptions: {
    mandate: new Date() }" />
```

 This example comes from a Stack Overflow answer by R. P. Niemeyer that can be found at http://stackoverflow.com/a/6400701/788260.

This binding's `init` function starts out by storing the jQuery wrapped element, followed by a check for options. The UI datepicker for jQuery (http://jqueryui. com/datepicker) has a lot of them, and letting the binding control the configuration is standard.

Next is the jQuery-fication of the element with `$el.datepicker(options)`. This attaches the event handlers that allow jQuery to hide and show the pop-up datepicker control and route its selection to the input element's `value`. Then, using Knockout's `ko.utils.registerEventHandler`, it attaches an event handler that takes the new `value` and writes it to the supplied observable.

In some cases, we might want to see whether the `valueAccessor` parameter is an observable, so that binding against a static value can still be used to set the element's initial value. You will want to use your best judgment here; in this case, the whole purpose of the binding is to collect user input, so it doesn't make sense in this case to work with nonobservable values. If you do want to make the check, you could change the event handler portion in the following manner:

```
if (ko.isObservable(valueAccessor())) {
    ko.utils.registerEventHandler(element, "change", function () {
        var observable = valueAccessor();
```

```
                observable($el.datepicker("getDate"));
        });
    }
```

The `ko.isObservable` function is a utility method that returns `true` if the first argument is an `observable`, `observableArray`, or `computed` observable. When the `valueAccessor` parameter isn't an observable, there is no need to attach the change handler at all, because there is nothing we would do with the new value.

The last piece in the `init` function is a **disposal handler**. Disposal of bindings occurs when the element is removed from the DOM, which happens when control flow bindings such as `template` or `foreach` update themselves. The `datepicker` control of jQuery expects `$el.datepicker("destroy")` to be called to clean up the event handlers if attached, and remove the pop-up element from the DOM. Remember, the pop-up element was added by jQuery from inside this binding handler, so Knockout's template system is not aware of them. The `ko.utils.domNodeDisposal.` `addDisposeCallback` registers handlers that will be called by the template system when it removes a node from the DOM. This is an important step anytime your binding handler has modified the DOM.

The `update` function handles observable changes, but as it is translating between strings for the element's value and JavaScript `Dates` for the code, it has to perform its own equality check. Instead of looking at the element's value, it uses `$el.datepicker("getDate")`, which returns a real JavaScript date.

To see this binding in action, you can check out the `cp2-datepicker` branch. I've added a `span` bound by the same viewmodel property as the datepicker so that you can easily see the value update.

# Modifying the DOM with bindings

The previous two bindings were mostly translators between the data and presentation logic, but binding handlers can do much more. Bindings can also be used to add new elements to the page. If you want to provide a UI for a 1-5 rating system, you should think about using a `select` element with an `options` and `value` binding. While this would work, a much more common way would be to provide a series of stars for the user to click on, with a click activating the clicked star and every previous star. The Knockout tutorial site (`http://learn.knockoutjs.` `com/#/?tutorial=custombindings`) provides a neat solution to this, which replaces a node's content with a list of styled `span` elements:

```
ko.bindingHandlers.starRating = {
    init: function(element, valueAccessor) {
        $(element).addClass("starRating");
        for (var i = 0; i < 5; i++) {
```

```
                $("<span>").appendTo(element);
    }

        // Handle mouse events on the stars
        $("span", element).each(function(index) {
            $(this).hover(
                function() {
                  $(this).prevAll().add(this)
                    .addClass("hoverChosen");
                },
                function() {
                  $(this).prevAll().add(this)
                    .removeClass("hoverChosen");
                }
            ).click(function() {
                var observable = valueAccessor();
                observable(index + 1);
            });
        });
    },
    update: function(element, valueAccessor) {
        // Give the first x stars the "chosen" class
        // where x <= rating
        var observable = valueAccessor();
        $("span", element).each(function(index) {
            $(this).toggleClass("chosen", index < observable());
        });
    }
};
```

You could use this binding on an element in the following manner:

```
<span data-bind="text: name"></span>
<span data-bind="starRating: rating"></span>
```

The result is a nice looking control that will be familiar to anyone who has filled out an online survey before:

The `init` function for this binding sets up three things. First, it adds five span elements as children of the bound node, which will serve as the stars for the rating. Second, it adds hover handlers to apply and remove the `hoverChosen` class to the star under the cursor, as well as all the previous stars. The stars are cumulative, so if we hover over the third star, we should see the first three stars fill in. Finally, it adds a click handler to each star that updates the `bound` property with the number the star represents. As its using the index of the loop, which starts at `0`, it adds `1` to the value. Again, we see that the binding assumes that the property being used is observable. If we wanted to support a read-only display, we would modify the binding to check that the property is observable before trying to update it.

The `update` function for this binding is different from the ones we've looked at so far. Instead of using the new value from the `valueAccesor` property to set an attribute of the original bound element, it loops through the stars and uses jQuery's `toggleClass` to set or remove the chosen class, applying it to only the stars whose index is at or below the new value. The viewmodel is still only aware of an integer value, and the view is only aware that the bound element is using `starRating` to present that number. The binding handler abstracts away star elements and also handles the translation between the numeric value and selected stars.

This binding assumes the existence of the CSS classes that it applies to the star spans. You can see an interactive sample of this binding and the CSS in the `cp2-stars` branch.

# Applying new bindings to new children elements

In the previous example, we looked at creating children elements to present our data with some style. It was using jQuery to manage the classes of the children elements that it had added during the binding's initialization. However, when using Knockout bindings, sometimes it makes more sense to use the built-in binding handlers for this sort of thing. Luckily it's possible to add Knockout bindings to elements after they've been created.

Knockout provides a utility function, `ko.applyBindingsToNode`, to manually apply bindings to elements. The function takes an element to bind an object. Each property on the object will be used to look up a binding handler, and the property's value will be passed to the binding. It also takes an optional viewmodel or binding context as the third parameter; if left out, it will use the current binding context:

```
init: function(element, valueAccessor) {
    var childElementToBind = document.createElement('input');
```

```
element.appendChild(childElementToBind);

ko.applyBindingsToNode(childElementToBind, {
  value: valueAccessor()
});
}
```

This will add a new input element after the original element and apply a `value` binding to the original observable. The `applyBindingsToNode` call takes the new input element and an object that will apply the `value` binding. The `valueAccessor` property returns the original property and passes it to the binding, essentially binding the new input to the same property as the original binding.

If we want to create a binding that adds an input with a new label, it might look like this:

```
ko.bindingHandlers.labelInput = {
    init: function(element, valueAccessor) {
        var input = document.createElement('input'),
          label = document.createElement('label'),
          labelText = valueAccessor().label,
          inputValue = valueAccessor().value;

        label.innerHTML = labelText;
        label.appendChild(input);

    element.appendChild(label);

    ko.applyBindingsToNode(input, {
      value: inputValue,
      valueUpdate: 'afterkeydown'
    });
    }
```

Its binding could be used as follows:

```
<div data-bind="labelInput: { label: 'Custom',
  value: name }"></div>
```

This binding creates a new label and input that it appends as children to the original binding. The label's text is set to the binding's `label` property, and the binding's `value` is bound to the input node. Hopefully, you can start to see how a binding handler could be used to create not only your own behavior, but your own custom elements as well.

An example of this binding can be seen in the `cp2-applynode` branch.

## Applying accessors

The `applyBindingsToNode` method is available in all versions of Knockout, but another method is available if you are using Knockout 3.0 or higher. The `applyBindingAccessorsToNode` method works in a way similar to `applyBindingsToNode`, taking an object to bind as the first parameter and an optional binding context as the third parameter. However, instead of taking the values of the second parameter's properties directly, it takes a function that supplies the `valueAccessor` property. The previous `apply` call would look like this after being converted:

```
ko. applyBindingAccessorsToNode (input, {
  value: function() { return inputValue },
  valueUpdate: function() { return 'afterkeydown' }
});
```

This method is actually what `applyBindingsToNode` calls internally after the values given to it are converted into value accessor functions such as the previous ones. The one fewer step of indirection gained by using `applyBindingAccessorsToNode` gives marginally improved performance. However, the larger benefit comes when the value being bound against it is an expression instead of just a simple property. An expression can only establish a dependency if it is evaluated from inside the binding that uses it. The value accessor functions will be evaluated later, allowing them to work correctly with expressions.

## Controlling the order of binding handlers

In rare cases, you may need to ensure that the binding handlers occur in a certain order. As of Knockout 3.0, this is possible by setting the `after` property on a binding handler to an array of bindings that must be processed first. For example, you can define a binding that require values and options to be processed first:

```
ko.bindingHandlers.valuePlus = {
    'after': ['options', 'value'],
    'init': function (element, valueAccessor, allBindings) {
        /* some code /*
      }
}
```

Several of the default bindings take advantage of this. The `value` binding depends on `options` and `foreach`; the `checked` binding depends on `value` and `attr`.

It should be noted that if you create two bindings with an `after` reference to each other, Knockout will throw a cyclic dependency exception if it ever tries to apply both bindings to the same element.

# Advanced binding handlers

So far, we've been looking at binding handlers that handle one or two properties and result in a fairly simple single-purpose control. In the previous example, we started looking at binding handlers that created new child elements, and this technique allows us to create much more complex binding behaviors. Bindings can also interact with complex elements such as charts or map controls (for example, a Google Maps widget), providing a clean API that the viewmodel can interact with.

# Binding complex data with charts

The first time we looked at integrating with a third-party control was with a single-property two-way binding to a datepicker. Any time we are working with third-party UI tools, the goal is to abstract them away from the view and the viewmodel through bindings; even when those tools are for complex structures such as charts.

Charts.js (http://www.chartjs.org) is a popular JavaScript library built to display data in, you guessed it right, graphical charts. Without going too deep into the details of how charts work, one challenge presented by a binding handler is that the chart doesn't have an API for making incremental updates. The whole chart needs to be re-rendered for updates. This requires access to the canvas element as well as the 2D context for the canvas. If we create the canvas in the init function, getting that element in the update function can be tricky. Let's take a look at an example of this (this is dummy code):

```
ko.bindingHandlers.doughnutChart = {
    init: function(element, valueAccessor) {
        var canvas = document.createElement('canvas'),
            options = ko.utils.extend(defaultChartOptions,
valueAccessor());

        element.appendChild(canvas);
    },
    update: function(element, valueAccessor) {
        var chartContext = canvas.getContext('2d')

        /* Drawing code */

        new Chart(chartContext).Doughnut(data, options);
    }
};
//HTML
<div data-bind="doughnutChart: {data: chartSeries}"></div>
```

You can see in the `init` function that a new canvas element has been made and appended to the bound element. However, the variable (`canvas`) needs to be used in the `update` function to draw, and it isn't actually available there.

Knockout provides two utility methods, `ko.utils.domData.set(element, key, value)` and `ko.utils.domData.get(element, key)`, which can be used to set values on the bound element. They can store any JavaScript value, including DOM node references, and so we could certainly use them here:

```
ko.bindingHandlers.doughnutChart = {
    init: function(element, valueAccessor) {
        var canvas = document.createElement('canvas'),
            options = ko.utils.extend(defaultChartOptions,
valueAccessor());

        ko.utils.domData.set(element, 'canvas', canvas);

        element.appendChild(canvas);
    },
    update: function(element, valueAccessor) {
        var canvas = ko.utils.domData.get(element, 'canvas'),
            chartContext = canvas.getContext('2d');

        /* Drawing code */

        new Chart(chartContext).Doughnut(data, options);
    }
};
```

This will work. However, it does mean that the element not only contains the canvas as a child, but also as a property; it also means the retrieval of the element every time an update runs.

Another method would be to create a computed observable in the `init` function that had a closure for the canvas, or even the context. This might sound like it's creating an extra object, but remember, the `update` function in bindings is actually wrapped in a computed to take advantage of the dependency detection. Using this method, our binding would look like this:

```
ko.bindingHandlers.doughnutChart = {
    init: function(element, valueAccessor) {
        var canvas = document.createElement('canvas'),
            options = ko.utils.extend(defaultChartOptions,
              valueAccessor()),
```

```
            chartContext = canvas.getContext('2d');

        element.appendChild(canvas);

        ko.computed(function() {
    canvas.height = ko.unwrap(options.height);
        canvas.width = ko.unwrap(options.width);

        var data = ko.toJS(options.data).map(function(x) {
          return {
            value: parseFloat(x.value),
            color: x.color.indexOf('#') === 0 ? "#" + x.color :
              x.color
          }
        });

        new Chart(chartContext).Doughnut(data, options);
      }, null, {disposeWhenNodeIsRemoved: element});
    }
  };
```

One thing to consider when using this method is the disposal of the computed. The third argument to the computed constructor is an options object, and with it, we can specify that the computed should be disposed off with a DOM node's removal by specifying the element. This option can be seen in the previous example.

Another thing to note in the example is the options variable in the init function. You should be familiar with the concept of extending objects, but just in case, remember that extending (also called merging) is the process of choosing a target and updating it with a source object by copying all of its properties. The result is an object with the combination of both values, with the values of the source being used in any cases where the target also had a value. Knockout provides an extend method on ko.utils.extend. I am using it here to make all of the chart options optional, by supplying these default values before the binding:

```
var defaultChartOptions = {
    height: 300,
    width: 300,
    animation: false
  };
```

The only thing that must be supplied is the data for the chart to display. Chart.js requires Doughnut charts to supply an array of objects with a value and color. To provide a humane binding, we can let the binding be responsible for ensuring the data is sanitized, which includes parsing the value as a number and ensuring our color value starts with the hash (#) for hex codes. Along with some options for height and width, our final computed would look something like this:

```
ko.computed(function() {

  canvas.height = ko.unwrap(options.height);
  canvas.width = ko.unwrap(options.width);

  var data = ko.toJS(options.data).map(function(x) {
    return {
      value: parseFloat(x.value),
      color: x.color.indexOf('#') === 0 ? x.color : "#" + x.color
    };
  });

  new Chart(chartContext).Doughnut(data, options);
}, null, {disposeWhenNodeIsRemoved: element});
```

An example of this binding, including some bindings to change the data, is in the cp2-charts branch.

## Dynamically adjusting the chart type

Three of the charts in Chart.js—Doughnut, Pie, and Polar Area—use the same data structure of value/color pairs. If you want to support switching between compatible charts, you can add the type as a binding option. The bottom of our computed would look like this instead:

```
var chart = new Chart(chartContext),
  chartType = ko.unwrap(options.type);

if (circularChartTypes.indexOf(chartType) === -1) {
  throw new Error('Chart Type ' + chartType + 'is not a Circular Chart
Type');
}

chart[chartType](data, options);
```

To indicate that this new binding supports multiple types, we could update the name and then use it like this:

```
<div data-bind="circularChart: {
            data: chartSeries,
            width: chartWidth,
            height: chartHeight,
            type: selectedChartType
}"></div>
```

This modified example can be seen in the `cp2-charts2` branch.

# Exposing APIs through bindings

The Chart.js example demonstrated binding against multiple properties. While we were able to control the chart by modifying bound observables for height, width, and type, it didn't allow us to *interact* with the chart. We could not click or drag the chart to update the observable for its data. The last custom binding technique we are going to look at is working with complex interactive controls; controls that bind multiple or complex data and allow user input. By doing this, we can consume APIs for a control either through the UI or programmatically. The example we will use is a binding for the Google Maps API.

One of our abstraction goals is to keep how the UI gets things done out of the declaration of the UI. It doesn't matter to us that the `visible` binding accomplishes its hiding by adding `style="display: none;"` to an element; all we care about is that the element will be visible only when the property we bind to is `truthy`.

Another goal of abstraction is to keep third-party data structures out of our viewmodel code, especially if that third-party code is only used by a binding handler. Our viewmodel doesn't care that its latitude and longitude are being used by a map, let alone a map from Google. That's the UI's business. However, it is still a fact of life that our data needs to be massaged into the correct format if we want it to play nicely with our third-party API. Here, again binding handlers come to the rescue!

The Google Maps JavaScript API is powerful and full of features. We are going to look at a simple binding that lets us control the center point of a map (latitude and longitude), as well as the zoom level of the map. We are going to hide all of the details of the Google Maps API inside our binding. Our viewmodel will be simple, just these three properties:

```
var BindingSample = function() {
  var self = this;
```

```
self.zoom = ko.observable(8);
self.latitude = ko.observable(45.51312335271636);
self.longitude = ko.observable(-122.67063820362091);
};
```

Hopefully, any reasonable mapping API would let us work with these properties, which allows our viewmodel to be reused for any of them. We want our HTML to be reusable as well, so it should use a map-provider agnostic syntax as well:

```
<div data-bind="map: { lat: latitude, long: longitude,
  zoom:zoom }" ></div>
```

So far so good; nothing new here. Let's take a look at that map binding handler:

```
ko.bindingHandlers.map = {
    init: function(element, valueAccessor) {
        var data = valueAccessor(),
            options = ko.utils.extend(ko.maps.defaults, data),
            //just get the relevant options
            mapOptions = {
                zoom: ko.unwrap(options.zoom),
                center: new google.maps.LatLng(ko.unwrap(options.lat),
                  ko.unwrap(options.long)),
                mapTypeId: options.mapType
            },
            map = new google.maps.Map(element, mapOptions);

        ko.computed(function() {
            map.setZoom(parseFloat(ko.unwrap(options.zoom)));
        }, null, { disposeWhenNodeIsRemoved: element });

        ko.computed(function() {
            map.panTo(new google.maps.LatLng(ko.unwrap(options.lat),
              ko.unwrap(options.long)));
        }, null, { disposeWhenNodeIsRemoved: element });

        google.maps.event.addListener(map, 'center_changed',
          function() {
            var center = map.getCenter();
            if (ko.isObservable(data.lat)) {
                data.lat(center.lat());
        }
            if (ko.isObservable(data.long)) {
                data.long(center.lng());
        }
        });
```

```
    if (ko.isObservable(data.zoom)) {
        google.maps.event.addListener(map, 'zoom_changed',
          function() {
            data.zoom(map.getZoom());
        });
    }
  }
};
```

The beginning should be familiar by now; we are getting our `valueAccessor` parameter out, using some default values (see the previous sample) and extending them with the bound data. The next line creates a new map using the Google Maps API and supplies the element and our options.

Next, we set up two computed values to update the map when the zoom or latitude/ longitude values change. Another advantage of using the computed method instead of the binding handlers `update` method is that the `update` method will fire when any part of the `valueAccessor` property changes. If only one value changes, such as zoom, we wouldn't want to update the map position. We would have to figure out which value changed, which would mean tracking it in the binding. Here, the two computed values will rerun only when their dependencies change, ensuring that we don't make unnecessary calls to update the map.

Finally, we have a pair of event listeners on the map to update our observable values when the user interacts with the map. These use the Google Maps API's `addListener` to get updates whenever the map is moved, which can happen by mouse dragging or with the keyboard arrows, and whenever the zoom is changed. The `panTo` function is just an animated `move` command; if the new position is close enough, `panTo` will ease into it.

That's it! If our code updates these values, the map will be moved. If the user moves the map, the bound observables will be updated. We have a two-way binding with multiple properties on a third-party UI control!

Obviously, this binding could get a lot bigger if we wanted to support more of the Google Maps APIs, but this should give you an idea of how that would be done. Don't be afraid to making larger bindings. The examples in this book are all small out of necessity — they tell me this will be printed on dead trees — but you should feel free to make bindings as large as you need to in order to accomplish the task at hand. I would take a larger, more flexible binding over a smaller inflexible binding any day.

If you want to see an example of this binding, check out the `cp2-maps` branch. It has several inputs bound to the map so that you can see things update in both directions. It's pretty fun to play with.

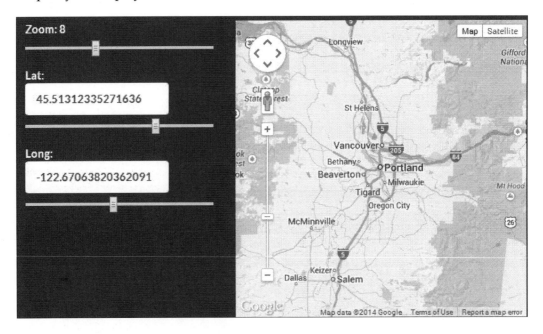

# Binding contexts and descendant bindings

All of the binding handlers we have created so far have respected the standard binding context. In this section, we are going to look at techniques to modify the binding context. This allows fine-grained control over how elements are bound and data they are bound with.

As per the Knockout documentation notes (`http://knockoutjs.com/documentation/custom-bindings-controlling-descendant-bindings.html`), these methods are not normally used in application development. They are probably only useful to library or framework developers building on top of Knockout.

# Controlling descendant bindings

You can indicate to Knockout that your binding handler is responsible for all of the bindings on descendant nodes by returning `controlsDescendantBindings` from the `init` function of a binding. The canonical example of this is the `stopBinding` handler:

```
ko.bindingHandlers.stopBinding = {
    init: function(element, valueAccessor) {
        return { controlsDescendantBindings:
ko.unwrap(valueAccessor()) };
    }
};
```

This will stop the current binding context from continuing to traverse these element descendants, leaving them in their initial unbound state unless another binding context is started:

```
<div data-bind="stopBinding: true">
  <h4 data-bind="text: 'Bound'">Unbound</h4>
</div>
```

The heading in this `div` element will still say Unbound after bindings are applied because `stopBinding` has stopped all descendant bindings. You can see an example of this binding in the `cp2-stopbinding` branch. Notice that if you change the `stopBinding` to `false`, the heading will say Bound.

So that's the basic idea, but what can we do with this? Well, after interrupting the current binding context, we can replace it with a different one!

# Child binding contexts

Probably the most common binding context operation is creating a child context, a context whose `$parent` is the current context. The `template`, `with`, and `foreach` bindings do this for the data they bind. A child context can access its parent using the special `$parent` property, and it can access the top-level viewmodel (the one passed to `ko.applyBindings`) by using `$root`. You can create your own child contexts by calling `createChildContext` on the `bindingContext` parameter passed to a binding handler.

Here is a binding that creates a child context by merging together two objects:

```
ko.bindingHandlers.merge = {
    init: function(element, valueAccessor, allBindings, viewmodel,
      bindingContext) {
```

```
        var value = valueAccessor(),
          merge = ko.utils.extend(value.target, value.source);
          child = bindingContext.createChildContext(merge);

    ko.applyBindingsToDescendants(child, element);

      // Don't bind the descendants
      return { controlsDescendantBindings: true };
    }
  };
```

This binding takes two properties, `target` and `source`, and uses the Knockout utility method `extend` to merge them together. Notice that because we are applying bindings to descendants, we have to return the `controlsDescendantBindings` flag. Consider the following viewmodel:

```
var BindingSample = function() {
    var self = this;
    self.name = 'Scout Retreat';
    self.springCourse = { knots: true, woodworking: true,
      metalworking: true };
    self.summerCourse = { rafting: true, diving: true, tracking:
      false };
};
```

We could use the `merge` binding to bind a template against the combined properties of the spring and summer courses:

```
<div data-bind="merge: { source: springCourse, target:
  summerCourse }">
  <h3 data-bind="text: $parent.name"></h3>
  <div>
    <label for="knots">Knots</label>
    <input type="checkbox" id="knots" disabled data-bind="checked:
      knots">
  </div>
  <div>
    <label for="woodworking">Woodworking</label>
    <input type="checkbox" id="woodworking"
      disabled data-bind="checked: woodworking">
<div>
    <label for="tracking">Tracking</label>
    <input type="checkbox" id="tracking"
      disabled data-bind="checked: tracking">
  </div>
```

```
    </div>
    <!-- More inputs -->
</div>
```

Notice that inside the merge binding, we can use `$parent.name` to get the viewmodel's name. Because the child binding was created from the binding context inside the merge binding handler, the original hierarchy is still accessible. You can see a working sample of this in the `cp2-mergecontext` branch.

# Extending binding contexts

It's possible to modify the current binding context without creating a new child in the hierarchy. Well, sort of. Extending the binding context clones the current context while adding properties at the same time. Other binding handlers, siblings or parents, won't be affected by this sort of change.

If we modify the previous example slightly, you can easily see the difference between extending and creating a child:

```
ko.bindingHandlers.merge = {
    init: function(element, valueAccessor, allBindings, viewmodel,
        bindingContext) {

        var value = valueAccessor(),
         merge = ko.utils.extend(value.target, value.source);
         context = bindingContext.extend(merge);

        ko.applyBindingsToDescendants(context, element);

        // Also tell KO *not* to bind the descendants itself,
           otherwise they will be bound twice
        return { controlsDescendantBindings: true };
    }
};
```

The only impact this has on the HTML binding is that the name no longer needs to call `$parent` first:

```
<div data-bind="merge: { source: springCourse, target:
    summerCourse }">
    <h3 data-bind="text: name"></h3>
```

You can see this example in the `cp2-mergecontext2` branch.

Extending and creating child contexts are very similar as far as potential use cases go. It's all going to depend on what you are doing, and whether or not adding layers is going to help. However, there is one more way of modifying the binding context, and it's a whole different beast.

## Setting a new $root context

In some situations, it may be desirable to create a new binding context hierarchy instead of adding a layer to the existing one. This would allow a binding handler to provide itself, or a context that it managed, as the `$root` binding context to any descendant bindings.

One use case for this would be a binding handler that used a recursive template:

```
var treeTemplate = '<div>Name:
  <span data-bind="text:name"></span><br>'
  +'Root: <span data-bind="text: isRoot ? \'Self\' :
    $root.name"></span><br>'
  +'<ul data-bind="foreach: { data: children, as: \'child\' }">'
    +'<li data-bind="tree: { data: child, children:
      $root.__children, name: $root.__name, isRoot: false
        }"></li>'
  +'</ul></div>';

ko.bindingHandlers.tree = {
    init: function(element, valueAccessor, allBindings, viewmodel,
      bindingContext) {

      var value = valueAccessor();
      var context = {
         __name: value.name,
         __children: value.children,
         //Default to true since template specifies
         isRoot: value.isRoot === undefined || value.isRoot,
         name: value.data[value.name],
         children: value.data[value.children],
      };

      element.innerHTML = treeTemplate;

      if (context.isRoot) {
          ko.applyBindings(context, element.firstChild);
    }
      else {
```

```
        ko.applyBindingsToDescendants(bindingContext.extend(context),
    element);
      }

      // Also tell KO *not* to bind the descendants itself,
        otherwise they will be bound twice
      return { controlsDescendantBindings: true };
    }
  };
```

This binding uses a recursive template to show an object and all of its children, while allowing the original binding to define the properties that will be used to populate this data. The root node's name is used on every descendant node using the `$root` binding context property, instead of having to walk back up the tree by counting the current depth. This is done with the call to `ko.applyBindings`, which unlike the other `apply` calls, creates an entirely new binding context using the first argument. Normally, this call is used to start applications, and when no second parameter is given, it applies to the entire window. The second parameter scopes this new context to the supplied element. The `tree` binding uses `firstChild` of the current element. Even though the `controlsDescendantBindings` flag stops Knockout from binding descendants, the current element is still bound, and applying bindings to it would cause the double-binding error to occur.

To use this binding, a viewmodel could start out with any self-same object, such as a person with children:

```
var BindingSample = function() {
   var self = this;

   self.person = {
      fullName: 'Alexander Hamilton',
      descendants: [ /* self-same children */]
   };
};
```

Then, use the `tree` binding to show this information without having to use a special viewmodel to match the properties:

```
<div data-bind="tree: {
               data: person,
               children: 'descendants',
               name: 'fullName'
}"></div>
```

This allows our `tree` binding to handle any recursive structure. You can see an example of this binding in the `cp2-rootcontext` branch.

# Containerless syntax with custom bindings

In the first chapter, we spoke about containerless bindings; bindings applied through comments that created a virtual container around their "child" nodes. Now that we have a good understanding of how to create our own binding handlers, it's time to learn how to make them containerless bindings.

First, we are going to make a normal binding and then look at what we need to do to allow it to support the virtual elements. Let's say you want a binding that sorts its children elements. It would need to loop through them, check some property, and then rearrange the DOM so they were in order. Normally, sorting would be achieved by using a `foreach` binding against a sorted `observableArray` property, but we're going to make a sort binding that sorts on the width of the DOM node, which takes into account any CSS that may have affected it. The viewmodel would have a hard time getting this information to determine the proper sort order, and HTML elements and widths don't belong in the viewmodel logic:

```
ko.bindingHandlers.widthSort = {
    init: function(element, valueAccessor) {
      // Pull out each of the child elements into an array
      var children = [];
      for (var i = element.children.length - 1; i >= 0; i--) {
        var child = element.children[i];
        //Don't take empty text nodes, they are not real nodes
        if (!isWhitespaceNode(child))
           children.push(child);
      };

      //Width calc must be done while the node is still in the DOM
      children.sort(function(a, b) {
         return $(a).width() <= $(b).width() ? -1 : 1;
      });

      while(children.length) {
         //Append will remove the node if it's already in the DOM
         element.appendChild(children.shift());
      }
    }
};
```

This binding would get used with a dummy property, as we aren't actually checking it:

```
<ul data-bind="widthSort: true">
```

The binding starts out by grabbing all the real child nodes from the bound element. The `isWhitespaceNode` check is just looking for the whitespace in the HTML from line breaks in between tags. We want to ignore these nodes because they will break the `with` check:

```
function isWhitespaceNode(node) {
    return !(/[^\t\n\r ]/.test(node.textContent))
            && node.nodeType == 3;
}
```

After grabbing the usable children from the element, it sorts them based on their width in the ascending order. Then, it loops through the sorted children and appends them to the bound element. Removal of nodes is automatic, as the DOM only allows a node to exist once. This produces our width-sorted list. You can see an example of this in the `cp2-sort` branch. It is used to sort the following list:

```
<ul data-bind="widthSort: true">
    <li>Jimmy Dean</li>
    <li>Sara Lee</li>
    <li>Famous Amos</li>
    <li>Orville Redenbacher</li>
    <li>Dr. Pepper</li>
</ul>
```

 Because the width sort uses the actual width in pixels, Orville Redenbacher ended up after The Kellogg brothers despite them being the same number of characters. Unless, of course, you are using a monospaced font.

# Using the virtual elements API

If you tried to use this binding as a virtual element binding right now, you would get an error telling you that it won't work. Knockout requires a flag to be set before bindings can be used in this way:

```
ko.virtualElements.allowedBindings.widthSort = true;
```

This flag tells Knockout that widthSort will work with virtual elements, so Knockout won't stop you from trying. It still won't work though, because our binding is making calls to the elements children. Comment nodes don't work with the normal JavaScript API, but Knockout provides a virtual element API that will work. These functions exist on the ko.virtualElements object:

- childNodes(containerElement): This returns the children of containerElement as an array.

- emptyNode(containerElement): This removes all children from containerElement. This also cleans any data attached to the node to prevent memory leaks.

- firstChild(containerElement): This returns the first child element, or null if the containerElement has no children.

- insertAfter(containerElement, nodeToInsert, insertAfter): This adds nodeToInsert to containerElement after the insertAfter node.

- nextSibling(node): This returns the next sibling of the node, or null if none exist.

- prepend(containerElement, nodeToPrepend): This inserts nodeToPrepend as the first child of containerElement.

- setDomNodeChildren(containerElement, arrayOfNodes): This removes any children from containerElement (cleaning attached data) before inserting arrayOfNodes as children.

All of these functions will treat a virtual element as if it were a real DOM node with children. They are also compatible with regular DOM nodes, so the same functions will work for regular and containerless bindings.

Updating the widthSort binding handlers to use this API would look like this:

```
ko.bindingHandlers.widthSort = {
    init: function(element, valueAccessor) {
        // Pull out each of the child elements into an array
        var children = [],
            childNodes = ko.virtualElements.childNodes(element);
        for (var i = childNodes.length - 1; i >= 0; i--) {
            var child = childNodes[i];
            //Don't take empty text nodes, they are not real nodes
            if (!isWhitespaceNode(child)) {
                children.push(child);
    }
    };
```

```
//Width calc must be done while the node is still in the DOM
children.sort(function(a, b) {
    return $(a).width() <= $(b).width() ? -1 : 1;
});

ko.virtualElements.setDomNodeChildren(element, children);
    }
};
```

The only two changes are using `childNodes` to get the children for sorting, and `setDomNodeChildren` to set the contents instead of looping through the sorted children. Our binding should now support the containerless syntax.

An example of the virtual elements version is in the `cp2-sort2` branch. For demonstration, the HTML has been updated so that the first element is not inside the sorting, something we couldn't have done without virtual element support:

```
<ul class="oddball clearfix">
    <li>Jimmy Dean</li>
    <!-- ko widthSort: true -->
    <li>Sara Lee</li>
    <li>Famous Amos</li>
    <li>Orville Redenbacher</li>
    <li>Johnny Appleseed</li>
    <li>The Kellog Brothers</li>
    <!-- /ko -->
</ul>
```

# Summary

If you take away one thing from all these examples, it should be that binding handlers are solely responsible for interaction with the DOM. In our first example, we made the `slideVisible` binding as an animated replacement for the standard `visible` binding. This change from the normal "instant" hide and show to the "animated" hide and show was completely decoupled by our viewmodel. This is beneficial because it keeps these two pieces completely separated, allowing them to develop and evolve independently.

In this chapter, we covered simple and complex binding handlers, binding context management, and using the virtual elements API to support containerless bindings. In the next chapter, we will be looking at preprocessors for bindings and nodes.

# 3
# Extending Knockout with Preprocessors and Providers

In the previous chapter, we looked at adding custom binding handlers to Knockout in order to add features and integrate them with third-party tools. This capability was part of Knockout when it was first released, and it allows for powerful extensions to Knockout's functionality. In this chapter, we are going to look at some more advanced techniques for extending, or even changing, Knockout binding behaviors. You will learn how to create:

- Binding handler preprocessors
- Node preprocessors
- Binding providers

After we cover this, we will take a look at the Knockout Punches library, which is a collection of preprocessors and extensions by Knockout developer Michael Best.

## Binding the handler preprocessing

So far, we have looked at two properties of binding handlers: the `init` and `update` functions. Binding handlers have another optional function, which is `preprocess`, that is run before the `init` function. A preprocessor's purpose is to modify the `data-binding` attribute before Knockout determines what bindings are to be applied.

Preprocessors don't deal with elements or binding contexts; they just deal with the strings that the binding will evaluate. For example, if we had a preprocessor that converts all text bindings to uppercase, then the following `span` element will be processed:

```
<span data-bind="text: 'That Guy'"></span>
```

This `span` element would be processed as if it was written like this:

```
<span data-bind="text: 'That Guy'.toUpperCase()"></span>
```

If you were to inspect the HTML after this, you will still see the original `data-bind` attribute. This is because preprocessors don't actually deal with elements; they just modify the binding strings before the normal binding handler is applied.

# Creating preprocessors

Adding a preprocessor is as simple as adding a `preprocess` property to the binding handler, just like we added the `init` and `update` functions:

```
ko.bindingHandlers.thing.preprocess = function(value, name,
  addBinding) {
    //Do stuff
}
```

The three parameters of the `preprocess` function are as follows:

- `value`: This is the expression given to the binding handler. For example, in `text: name`, the value is `name`; for `text: title() + '. ' + name()`, the value is `"title() + '. ' + name()"`. This value is always a string.

- `name`: This is the name of the binding handler, for example, `text` or `click`. This can be useful in cases where a single `preprocess` function is used by multiple binding handlers.

- `addBinding`: This is a callback function that takes the `name` and `value` string parameters, just like the previous ones. It will add the pair as a binding on the element.

The return value from the preprocessor will be the new value used for the entire binding.

Let's look at a few examples.

# The uppercase preprocessor

The Knockout documentation provides an example for this preprocessor that, at the time of writing this, returns `value + ".toUpperCase()"`. The full preprocessor will look like this:

```
ko.bindingHandlers.text.preprocess = function(value) {
  return value + '.toUpperCase()';
};
```

The preceding code would work, for example, at the beginning of this section when it took a string directly:

```
<span data-bind="text: 'That Guy'"></span>
```

The result of our preprocessor will be `text: 'That Guy'.toUpperCase()` and the text binding will handle this without any error. Unfortunately, this will break in the normal case of binding against observable properties:

```
<span data-bind="text: firstName"></span>
```

Knockout's normal binding process unwraps the expression it gets so that observables don't need parentheses. Preprocessors, on the other hand, just output strings that are directly consumed by the binding handler. Our uppercase binding will produce an illegal result here:

```
<span data-bind="text: firstName.toUpperCase()"></span>
```

This will fail, as `firstName` is an observable and not a string, and observables don't have a `toUpperCase` method.

Luckily, the solution to this is simple. Our preprocessor can safely handle all value expressions by applying an `unwrap` function to the output:

```
ko.bindingHandlers.text.preprocess = function(value) {
    return 'ko.unwrap(' + value + ').toUpperCase()';
};
```

This will ensure that any value—whether a primitive type, observable, or inline expression—is correctly evaluated by the binding handler.

You can see an example of this preprocessor in the `cp3-uppercase` branch.

# Wrapping existing bindings

Because Knockout provides default bindings for most standard scenarios, it's common to want for a custom binding to build on top of them. Preprocessors make wrapping other bindings very easy.

Let's say that we wanted a binding that caused an element to flash when a property was updated in addition to providing a `value` binding on it. Normally, you might want to divide these into two separate bindings, but if you are doing this a lot, a single binding will save time and keystrokes.

As the `value` binding already exists, we can just use a preprocessor to add the binding with the `addBinding` callback:

```
ko.bindingHandlers.valueFlash = {
  preprocess: function(value, name, addBinding) {
      addBinding('value', value);
      return value;
  },
  update: function(element, valueAccessor) {
      ko.unwrap(valueAccessor());   //unwrap to get dependency
      $(element).css({opacity: 0}).animate({opacity: 1}, 500);
  }
};
```

The `addBinding` callback takes care of generating the `value` binding as if it had been applied normally, which includes running the preprocessor for the new binding (if it has one).

It's important that we still return the original value after adding the `value` binding. If nothing is returned from the `preprocess` function, then the original binding is removed. After this, the rest of the binding handler is business as usual: add an `init` and `update` function (as required) and write your custom behavior. There is an example of this binding in the `cp3-wrap` branch.

That's really all there is to creating binding handler preprocessors. For the extensibility they allow, they are simple and straightforward to use. We will look at some more real-world possibilities for binding preprocessors when we look at `Knockout.Punches` in the last section of this chapter.

# Node preprocessors

Binding handler preprocessors are attached to individual binding handlers and work by modifying the binding string. They only apply to nodes of their respective handler.

Node preprocessors, on the other hand, are called on every DOM node. They run when the UI is first bound and when it is modified by bindings such as `foreach` or `template`.

The purpose of a node preprocessor is to modify the DOM before data-binding occurs, as opposed to a binding preprocessor that only modifies the `data-bind` attribute. A node preprocessor is defined by adding a `preprocessNode` function to the binding provider:

```
ko.bindingProvider.instance.preprocessNode = function(node) {
  /* DOM code */
}
```

A preprocessor is called once for each node. If no changes need to be made, it should return nothing. Otherwise, it can use the standard DOM API to insert new nodes or remove the current node:

- New nodes should be inserted before the current node by using:

  ```
  node.parentNode.insertBefore(newNode, node);
  ```

- Replacement can be done with:

  ```
  node.parentnode.replaceChild(newNode, node);
  ```

- Removal can be done with:

  ```
  node.parentNode.removeChild(node);
  ```

Any nodes that are added need to be returned from `preprocessNode`; otherwise, Knockout will not apply bindings to them. As you do not have the binding context inside `preprocessNode` (you only have the current node), it is not possible to apply bindings yourself, unless they are applied to constant or global values. This is not recommended, though, as it creates a new binding context outside of the current context's hierarchy.

# Closing virtual template nodes

The Knockout documentation provides a handy node preprocessor that self-closes virtual template bindings. Normally, when writing a containerless template binding, you would need two comment nodes:

```
<!-- template: 'some-template' --><!-- /ko -->
```

As a template binding never contains content when referencing an external template, the closing comment node feels unnecessary. A `preprocess` function will allow you to use a template without the closing tag so that you can write the binding like this:

```
<!-- template: 'some-template' -->
```

Knockout requires a closing comment tag, which is `<!-- /ko -->`, for virtual bindings. We can provide this comment node automatically with a preprocessor:

```
ko.bindingProvider.instance.preprocessNode = function(node) {
    if (node.nodeType == node.COMMENT_NODE) {
        var match = node.nodeValue.match(/^\s*(template\s*:[\s\S]+)/);
        if (match) {
            // Create a pair of comments to replace the single comment
            var c1 = document.createComment("ko " + match[1]),
                c2 = document.createComment("/ko");
            node.parentNode.insertBefore(c1, node);
            node.parentNode.replaceChild(c2, node);

            // Tell Knockout about the new nodes so that it can apply
bindings to them
            return [c1, c2];
        }
    }
};
```

This sample uses regex to identify template comments and extract the expression from the binding. Then, it replaces the original comment with the standard open/close pair of comments for a virtual template binding. Finally, it returns the new comment nodes, allowing Knockout to bind them; this will apply the template to the virtual container created by the comment nodes.

# Supporting alternate syntaxes

The previous example should have given you an idea of how node preprocessors work. However, the real power of node preprocessors comes from letting us extend the data binding syntax itself.

It's not uncommon to see a series of text bindings like this one:

```
First Name: <!-- text: firstName --><!-- /ko -->
Last Name: <!-- text: lastName  --><!-- /ko -->
Birth Date: <!-- text: birthDate --><!-- /ko -->
```

We want to list out several properties, but these virtual elements are pretty verbose. On top of the property name, they add 29 characters, including spaces. We can also use `span` elements, of course, but they are about the same size, considering that they need the `data-bind` attributes in addition to the binding name.

If you've ever used AngularJS or Handlebars, you'll probably appreciate the minimal requirement of using curly braces to access values as strings. The preceding example will look like this:

```
First Name: {{ firstName }}
Last Name: {{ lastName }}
Birth Date: {{ birthDate }}
```

Look how much shorter and easier to read this is! These Handlebars guys have the right idea. I'm sure you know where we are going with this. A node preprocessor will allow us to take this same HTML and replace it with the HTML from the first example.

This example is long, so we are going to break it up a bit:

```
var expressionRegex = /{{([\s\S]+?)}}/g;
ko.bindingProvider.instance.preprocessNode = function(node) {
    if (node.nodeType === 3 && node.nodeValue) {
        var newNodes = //Collect new nodes by scanning "node"

        // Insert the resulting nodes into the DOM
        // remove the original unprocessed node
        if (newNodes) {
            for (var i = 0; i < newNodes.length; i++) {
                node.parentNode.insertBefore(newNodes[i], node);
            }
            node.parentNode.removeChild(node);
            return newNodes;
        }
    }
};
```

First, we have a regex pattern that finds these double curly brace chunks. As text nodes will contain any content up to the first real element they encounter, its possible that multiple curly brace chunks might be in a single node, so it needs to match globally. Then, the `preprocess` function starts out by checking for the text node type.

I've omitted the section that actually scans the node to create new ones for now; we will come back to that in just a bit.

If we have any nodes that need to be added, they get inserted, and then the original node is removed. Finally, the nodes we inserted are returned so that Knockout can bind them.

This is almost boilerplate code for node preprocessors, and it's a very good pattern to follow. Check for a type, create any new nodes, replace the original nodes if there are any, and return the new nodes. If you are creating a node preprocessor, this is a good template to start with.

Okay, let's get to the meat. To assign `newNodes`, we need to check the node for our regex pattern and build a pair of virtual text bindings for each match:

```
var newNodes = replaceExpressionsInText(node.nodeValue,
    expressionRegex, function(expressionText) {
      return [
          document.createComment("ko text:" + expressionText),
          document.createComment("/ko")
      ];
});
```

Here, we are calling `replaceExpressionsInText` and passing the node's contents, our regex pattern, and a callback that builds the correct replacements with the expression found by our regex. Then, we just need the actual search:

```
function replaceExpressionsInText(text, expressionRegex, callback) {
    var prevIndex = expressionRegex.lastIndex = 0,
        resultNodes = null,
        match;

    while (match = expressionRegex.exec(text)) {
        var leadingText = text.substring(prevIndex, match.index);
        prevIndex = expressionRegex.lastIndex;
        resultNodes = resultNodes || [];

        // Preserve leading text
        if (leadingText) {
            resultNodes.push(document.createTextNode(leadingText));
        }

        resultNodes.push.apply(resultNodes, callback(match[1]));
    }

    // Preserve trailing text
    var trailingText = text.substring(prevIndex);
    if (resultNodes && trailingText) {
        resultNodes.push(document.createTextNode(trailingText));
    }

    return resultNodes;
}
```

The search function loops on the regex pattern and pulls out the first match. It sends the match to the callback function and keeps the result, along with any leading or trailing spaces. When it's finished matching, it returns them.

That's it. Now, our Handlebars code will be converted to virtual text bindings. You can see this example in the `cp3-interpolate` branch.

> This code is adapted from the `StringInterpolatingBindingProvider` demo at http://blog.stevensanderson.com/2013/07/09/.

## Multiple syntaxes

If we wanted to push this example a bit farther, we could support additional interpolation syntaxes. `replaceExpressionsInText` is already set up to take regex input, and as it uses a callback, we can even construct nodes differently for different regex patterns.

Let's add the embedded Ruby syntax interpolation, which uses `<%= expression %>`:

```
// Replace <%= expr %> with data bound span's
var erbNodes = replaceExpressionsInText(node.nodeValue,
/\<\%=([\s\S]+?)\%\>/g, function(expressionText) {
    var span = document.createElement('span');
    span.setAttribute('data-bind', 'text: ' + expressionText);
    return [span];
});
```

This time, we are replacing a `span` element instead of a virtual text element so that we can tell the resulting HTML apart. As this preprocessor can support both syntaxes, you can bind against a mixed syntax template:

```
First Name: {{ firstName }}
Last Name: <%= lastName %>
Birth Date: {{ birthDate }}
```

The resulting HTML will look like this:

```
First Name: <!--ko text: firstName --><!--/ko-->
Last Name: <span data-bind="text: lastName"></span>
Birth Date: <!--ko text: birthDate --><!--/ko-->
```

You can see this example in the `cp3-interpolate2` branch.

# Binding providers

With a binding preprocessor, we have access to the binding expression and can modify it before the evaluation of bindings. With a node preprocessor, we have access to the node and can modify the DOM before bindings are applied. Both of these just transform things into the normal Knockout syntax. They are also limited to operating on the DOM, and they do not have access to the binding context.

Knockout binding providers are objects that receive both the DOM node and the binding context and determine which bindings handlers will be applied and what `valueAccessor` properties those bindings receive.

A binding provider is expected to provide the following functions:

- `nodeHasBindings(node)`: This function should return a Boolean that indicates whether or not the node has any bindings defined on it.
- `getBindingAccessors(node, bindingContext)`: This function should return an object with a property for each binding to be applied whose value is a function that evaluates the binding expression. This function is used as the `valueAccessor` property in binding handlers.

 If you are targeting 2.x, you will need to support `getBindings`, which returns an object whose property values are the final binding values. This function was deprecated with Knockout 3.0.

The default binding provider operates by looking for `data-bind` attributes on an element or a comment node that starts with `ko`. If it does, `nodeHasBindings` will return `true`. When `getBindingAccessors` is called, it returns the bindings by evaluating the `data-bind` attribute and getting the `valueAccessors` property from the binding context.

# Custom binding providers

We've already seen how we can use preprocessors to allow for different syntaxes to be used for data binding. So, to get a better understanding of the capability of binding providers, we are going to look at something preprocessors can't do: choosing bindings based on the data type.

The Knockout plugin `Knockout.BindingConventions` (`https://github.com/ AndersMalmgren/Knockout.BindingConventions`) creates a binding provider that provides bindings on the `data-name` attribute by looking at the binding context for clues on the bindings that are to be used, which makes it a great example for a custom provider. As this is a big change from how Knockout works, let's compare this to a standard viewmodel and binding setup:

```
var BindingSample = function() {
   var self = this;

   self.name = ko.observable('Timothy');
   self.locations = ['Portland', 'Seattle', 'New York City'];
   self.selectedLocation = ko.observable();
   self.isAdmin = ko.observable(true););
};
```

Binding to this with standard Knockout bindings might look something like this:

```
<label>Name
   <input data-bind="value: name" />
</label>
<label>LocationLocationName
   <select data-bind="options: locations, value: selectedLocation"></select>
</label>
<label>Admin
   <input data-bind="checked: isAdmin" type="checkbox" />
</label>
```

We've got three bound elements and four bindings. The first input is a `value` that is binding to `name`, the `select` element is binding to `options` on `locations` and `value` on `selectedLocation`, and the last input is binding `checked` to `isAdmin`. A simple case, such as having to specify that the binding on an input is a value, might seem verbose; in most cases, an input will be binding against the value, or in the case of a checkbox, binding against `checked`.

The convention-over-configuration philosophy aims to remove the need to specify what is happening in a conventional scenario. In other words, perform the standard action unless otherwise specified. Here is how the previous DOM would look using the `BindingConventions` plugin:

```
<label>Name
   <input data-name="name" />
</label>
<label>LocationNameLocation
```

```
    <select data-name="locations"></select>
  </label>
  <label>Admin
    <input data-name="isAdmin" />
  </label>
```

Here, `BindingConventions` is doing all the work of figuring out the bindings. The `name` input is a string observable on our viewmodel, and it's on an input node, so it gets the `value` binding. The `isAdmin` input is a Boolean observable on our viewmodel, so the input node is converted into a checkbox, and it receives the `checked` binding. The `locations` property is an array on our viewmodel, so the `select` element gets an `options` binding. However, this is not all! Our viewmodel has a `selectedLocations` observable, which `BindingConventions` determines should get a `value` binding for the `select` element, as singularizing an array name and prepending `selected` is a binding convention.

That last one might seem like magic, and personally, I think it's a bit too non-obvious, but it has a certain appeal to it. If you are following conventions, you can really simplify your bindings. You can see this example in action in the `cp3-provider` branch.

Now that you can see what this binding provider is doing, let's look at how it works.

 We will be looking at a simplified version of the binding provider in the `BindingConventions` plugin. The real provider supports more conventions and allows for custom conventions to be added. This sample is only meant to illustrate the type detection concept and the basics of creating a custom provider.

The first thing that needs to be decided when creating a custom binding provider is whether you need to extend the default binding provider or replace it. The `BindingConventions` provider will support the `data-name` attribute. In this case, it makes sense to extend the default provider, as they do not conflict with each other and we will need the standard `data-bind` support for scenarios that are nonconventional (such as binding our select value to a `favoriteLocation` property).

The easiest way to do this is to store a reference to the original binding provider and call it in our custom provider:

```
ko.bindingConventions = {};
ko.bindingConventions.ConventionBindingProvider = function () {
    this.orgBindingProvider = ko.bindingProvider.instance || new
      ko.bindingProvider();
};
```

```
var nodeHasBindings = function(node) { /* check node */ };
var conventionBindings = function(node, bindingContext) { /* check
node
  */ };

 ko.bindingConventions.ConventionBindingProvider.prototype = {
     nodeHasBindings: function (node) {
         return this.orgBindingProvider.nodeHasBindings(node) ||
           nodeHasBindings(node);
     },
     getBindingAccessors: function (node, bindingContext) {
         return this.orgBindingProvider.getBindingAccessors
           (node, bindingContext)
             || conventionBindings(node, bindingContext);
     }
 };
 ko.bindingProvider.instance =
   new ko.bindingConventions.ConventionBindingProvider();
```

This is basically boilerplate for a binding provider that extends the default
one. It stores the original provider and implements the `nodeHasBindings` and
`getBindingAccessors` functions by calling the default provider first, calling its own
implementation if the default provider returns nothing. If you want your provider
to check for bindings before the default one, you can switch the order of the calls.
Finally, you can combine the two by appending binding handlers to the result of
the default provider.

After setting up the required functions, `ko.bindingProvider.instance` is replaced
with the new custom provider. It's important to note that this must all be done prior
to `ko.applyBindings` being called, as the binding provider is only constructed once
for the root binding context.

From here, all we have to do is provide the methods that check for bindings
and create them. Checking for bindings just requires you to check for the
`data-name` attribute:

```
var getNameAttribute = function (node) {
   var name = null;
   if (node.nodeType === 1) {
      name = node.getAttribute("data-name");
   }
   return name;
};

var nodeHasBindings = function(node) {
   return getNameAttribute(node) !== null;
};
```

Getting the value from the binding context is a bit more work. Knockout has utility methods that can parse expressions under the `ko.expressionRewriting` object, which can read any of the supported Knockout binding syntaxes. The `BindingConventions` plugin does not support anything other than property references, but it does support deep references such as `person.firstName`. For simplicity's sake, I am not going to cover this, but if you are interested in this, you can look at `getDataFromComplexObjectQuery` in the plugin's source code. For now, we will assume that all `data-name` attributes refer directly to a property:

```
var conventionBindings = function(node, bindingContext) {
    var bindings = {};
    var name = getNameAttribute(node);
    if (name === null) {
        return null;
}

    var data = bindingContext[name] ? bindingContext[name] :
        bindingContext.$data[name];

    if (data === undefined) {
        throw "Can't resolve member: " + name;
    }

    var unwrapped = ko.utils.peekObservable(data);
    var type = typeof unwrapped;

    //Loop through convention handlers to construct bindings

    return bindings;
};
```

First, we get the name of the viewmodel property from the `data-name` attribute, and then we perform a sanity check to make sure that it's there to bind against. Then, we get the data with `ko.utils.peekObservable` and check its type. All observables have a `peek` function that returns the underlying value without triggering dependency detection. The `peekObservable` function will call `peek` if the first parameter is observable; otherwise, it will just return the first parameter. It's a safety utility that is similar to `ko.uwrap`.

After we have these two bits of information, we can build the binding object we need to return. Remember, this binding object should have a property named after the binding to be applied, whose value is the `valueAccessor` object for the binding. The bindings are returned to the binding provider's `getBindingAccessors` function. To construct the bindings, we will loop over a set of conventions:

```
for (var index in ko.bindingConventions.conventionBinders) {
    if (ko.bindingConventions.conventionBinders
        [index].rules !== undefined) {
```

```
    var convention =
      ko.bindingConventions.conventionBinders[index];
    var shouldApply = true;

    convention.rules.forEach(function (rule) {
       shouldApply = shouldApply && rule(name, node, bindings,
          unwrapped, type, data, bindingContext);
    });

    if (shouldApply) {
       convention.apply(name, node, bindings, unwrapped, type,
          function() { return data }, bindingContext);
       break;
    }
  }
}
```

This will look through the `conventionBinders` array and check the rules for each one in order to find a match for the current node, data, and data type. If all of the rules for a convention handler pass, then we call `apply` for that convention and stop checking—only one convention should apply per node. The `apply` function gets all of the information we've collected so far as well as a `valueAccessor` property that can be used for the binding.

Our example is only using two conventions, which are `options` and `input`:

```
ko.bindingConventions.conventionBinders.options = {
  rules: [function (name, element, bindings, unwrapped) { return
    element.tagName === 'SELECT' && unwrapped.push; } ],
  apply: function (name, element, bindings, unwrapped, type,
    valueAccessor, bindingContext) {
     bindings.options = valueAccessor;
     singularize(name, function (singularized) {
        var selectedName = 'selected' +
          getPascalCased(singularized);
        if (bindingContext.$data[selectedName] !== undefined) {
           bindings['value'] = function() {
              return bindingContext.$data[selectedName];
           };
        }
     });
  }
};
```

The options have just one rule: the element must be a `select` element, and the data needs to be an array (which is being checked by looking for a `push` function).

The `apply` function sets the options binding directly to the `valueAccessor` property. Then, it tries to find a property that matches the `'selected'` + `getPascalCased(singularized)` convention on the context. The `singularize` and `getPascalCased` functions are not included here, but you can see them in the example branch in the following code. Predictably, they find a singular conjugation of a word and capitalize the first letter. If a match is found, a `value` binding is added to the `bindings` object that was passed in.

The `input` handler is much simpler:

```
ko.bindingConventions.conventionBinders.input = {
  rules: [function (name, element) { return element.tagName ===
    'INPUT' || element.tagName === 'TEXTAREA'; } ],
  apply: function (name, element, bindings, unwrapped, type,
    valueAccessor, bindingContext) {
      var bindingName = null;
      if (type === 'boolean') {
          element.setAttribute('type', 'checkbox');
          bindingName = 'checked';
      } else {
          bindingName = 'value';
      }
      bindings[bindingName] = valueAccessor;
  }
};
```

The `input` handler's rules don't check the data type; it's just that the node is either `input` or `textarea`. The `apply` function will use a `value` binding if the type is not `Boolean`; otherwise, it sets the `checkbox` property on the node and uses the `checked` binding.

That's it. This binding provider will allow binding to occur with the `data-name` attribute, requiring only a view model property as the value, and it intelligently sets up bindings for the conventional scenario. If we need more control, the regular `data-bind` attributes can still be used to apply bindings.

This simplified implementation of the `BindingConventions` binding provider can be seen in the `cp3-provider2` branch. The `client/app` directory in the branch contains both the simplified implementation discussed here as well as the full implementation from the plugin.

None of this would be possible with a binding or node preprocessor, as it relies on the type of data from the binding context. Hopefully, this will give you a good idea of what is possible with custom binding providers and the flexibility of the overall binding system.

# Knockout punches

Now that you are familiar with the techniques that are used to modify the binding syntax and the general use of preprocessors, we are going to look at the popular Knockout plugin `Knockout.Punches` (get it?). Punches is written by Michael Best, who is a Knockout developer and the creator of the Knockout preprocessor functionality and some of the best real-world use cases for preprocessors. We are going to look at some of them and dig in to see how they work. This section is not going to cover everything in Knockout Punches; if you want to learn more about it, you can check out the documentation online.

 The documentation for `Knockout.Punches` can be found at `http://mbest.github.io/knockout.punches`, which includes an API reference and the source code.

# Embedded text bindings

Embedded text bindings offer the same syntax that we created with the preprocessor in the *Supporting alternate syntaxes* section—converting curly braces into virtual text nodes:

```
<div>Hello {{ name }}.</div>
```

The previous command becomes the following:

```
<div>Hello <!--ko text:name--><!--/ko-->.</div>
```

The method Knockout Punches uses is more performant than the one we looked at, but it still offers the same customizability we used. If you want to use something besides virtual text nodes as the interpolation replacement, you can provide your own `node-array` returning function as a replacement for the following:

```
ko.punches.utils.interpolationMarkup.wrapExpression(expressionText)
```

# Namespaced bindings

Knockout Punches offers a shorthand binding syntax that expands `x.y: value` to `x : { y: value }`. By default, this namespace syntax is available for the `event`, `attr`, `style`, and `css` bindings. Using it on the `style` binding will cause the following to expand:

```
<div data-bind="style.color: textColor"></div>
```

This will expand to the following:

```
<div data-bind="style: { color: textColor }"></div>
```

This works by overriding the standard `ko.getBindingHandler` function, which just returns the binding handler normally. It is replaced by one that looks for a dot in the name of the binding with a matching `getNamespacedHandler` property and returns that one instead.

# Dynamic namespaced bindings

Because `ko.getBindingHandler` is overridden like this, it is possible to create your own binding namespaces by adding a `getNamespacedHandler` property to a binding handler:

```
ko.bindingHandlers.customNamespace = {
    getNamespacedHandler: function(binding) {
        return {
            init: function(element, valueAccessor) { },
            update: function(element, valueAccessor) { }
        };
    }
};
```

The `binding` argument is the name of the binding; for `style.color`, it will be `color`. The function returns the binding handler to be used. This allows you to provide a single dynamic handler for all bindings in a namespace.

Let's say that we want to create a binding namespace for the Twitter Bootstrap tooltip plugin. We need to supply the text contents and the direction of the tooltip. Normally, we might write a binding that took each of these as options:

```
ko.bindingHandlers.tooltip = {
    update: function(element, valueAccessor) {
        //Cleanup previous tooltips
        if (element.attributes['data-original-title']) {
            $(element).tooltip('destroy');
        }
```

```
        var options = valueAccessor();
          $(element).tooltip({
            placement: options.placement || 'left',
            title: ko.unwrap(options.title || 'sample')
          });
      }
    };
```

Then, we could bind on it with an object:

```
data-bind="tooltip: { placement: 'top', title: title}"
```

This works fine, but we can rewrite this using a namespaced binding handler in order to get the dot syntax for the placement:

```
ko.bindingHandlers.tooltip = {
    getNamespacedHandler: function(binding) {
        return {
            update: function(element, valueAccessor) {
              //Cleanup previous tooltips
              if (element.attributes['data-original-title']) {
                $(element).tooltip('destroy');
      }

                $(element).tooltip({
                  placement: binding,
                  title: ko.unwrap(valueAccessor())
                });
            }
        };
    }
};
```

This produces a much shorter binding attribute, which I think is easier to read:

```
data-bind="tooltip.top: title"
```

An example of this can be seen in the `cp3-namespace` branch.

# Binding filters

It's pretty common to perform filtering on viewmodel properties. The usual practice is to have a computed property on the viewmodel perform the filtering, but this can become verbose, especially if you have several different filtered properties. Knockout Punches provides syntax that applies filter expressions inside of bindings:

```
<span data-bind="text: name | fit:20 | uppercase"></span>
```

Filters are pipe-delimited, and multiple arguments are separated by colons. For example, `fit` takes up to three arguments, which can be specified with `fit:20:'...':'middle'`.

It should be noted that `name` does not include the observable parentheses in the preceding example. While the entire binding with the filters is a single expression, which would normally require the parentheses, Knockout Punches intelligently handles each section by calling `ko.unwrap` on it. This means that the binding value and each filter are treated as their own expression.

Filtering is accomplished with a binding preprocessor that parses the expression and recursively unwraps the piped sections into a call to the filter. The preceding example will end up returning the following from the `preprocess` function:

```
ko.filters['uppercase'](ko.filters['fit'](name,20))
```

# Writing custom filters

Adding your own filters is very similar to adding binding handlers. Just add a function to the `ko.filters` object that takes a value and any number of arguments and returns a modified value:

```
ko.filters.translate = function(value, language) {
    return SomeLanguageLibrary.translate(value, language);
}
```

The first argument is the current value that is to be processed. All other arguments are those that are given to the filter in the binding expression.

Filters can have zero arguments—as in the `uppercase` example—or optional arguments—as in the `fit` example. The filter preprocessor does not check the filter to see whether the number of arguments it's sending make sense; it just calls the filter with everything in the binding expression.

The filter preprocessor is simple to extend, and it offers considerable power. I think it is one of the best examples anywhere of the potential of binding preprocessors.

# Filters on other bindings

By default, filters are enabled for the `text`, `attr`, and `html` bindings, but additional bindings can use filters by calling `ko.punches.textFilter.enableForBinding(<binding>)`. This can be useful if you wanted to take advantage of filters on a custom binding.

Filters cannot be used in two-way bindings, such as the binding value, as they always produce inline expressions.

# Adding additional preprocessors

Knockout Punches provides two utility methods in order to add additional binding and node preprocessors that can be accessed from `ko.punches.utils`:

- `addBindingPreprocessor(bindingKeyOrHandler, preprocessFn)`
- `addNodePreprocessor(preprocessFn)`

If you call either of these multiple times, the respective preprocessors will be chained together, with each new preprocessor being called at the end of the chain.

The binding preprocessors will run until one of them removes the binding or until the end of the chain is reached. This stops the chain from trying to process a binding that no longer exists.

The node preprocessors will run until one of them returns new nodes to add or until the end of the chain is reached. This stops the chain from trying to process a node that has already been modified. The new nodes will not be walked by the node preprocessors, so they should be added to the DOM and be made ready for data binding.

# Summary

This chapter was all about how to extend Knockout's binding process and modify its syntax. We covered three ways of doing this:

- **Binding Preprocessors**: This is used to modify binding strings before binding handlers run
- **Node Preprocessors**: This is used to modify the DOM before the binding starts
- **Binding Providers**: This is used to control what bindings are applied to each DOM node

Finally, we looked at the `Knockout.Punches` plugin to see some real-world Knockout extensions.

In the next chapter, we will cover Knockout's web component features, which let you tie view and viewmodel together into reusable controls.

# 4

# Application Development with Components and Modules

Okay, time to get back to application development. We touched briefly on this back in *Chapter 1, Knockout Essentials*; we will be returning to it here. This chapter is all about how to work with Knockout inside modern web applications. In this chapter, we will look at the following topics:

- Using modules with RequireJS
- Creating reusable components
- Extending Knockout with custom component loaders
- **Single Page Application (SPA)** routing

Because Knockout is a library—a fact it proclaims proudly on the home page—it doesn't cover everything you need in complete web applications. This allows Knockout to specialize by focusing on a limited feature set, but it leaves the task of deciding how to build the rest of the application to you, the developer. The methods we cover in this chapter are not the only available options—we don't have that kind of time or space—but they should provide enough general guidance to help you make your own decisions while keeping in mind Knockout's strengths.

We are also going to transform the `Contacts List` application to an SPA—an application that uses JavaScript to change the template of the current view, mimicking a page change instead of using browser navigation. This pattern has become so popular that most developers consider it a given when working on new JavaScript web clients, so it's important to understand how Knockout fits into this model of development.

# RequireJS – AMD viewmodels

RequireJS (`http://requirejs.org/`) is a library that you should have at least heard of already, if not used. This is still a book about Knockout, and if you are planning to use RequireJS in an application, you should read up on it first, but I will still give you a brief overview here.

## An overview of RequireJS

RequireJS's purpose is to allow your code to be broken into modules that declare their dependencies so that they can be injected at runtime. This has several important benefits. As RequireJS loads your JavaScript, you don't have to include each script with a `script` tag in your HTML. As RequireJS loads the scripts based on their dependencies, you don't have to worry about the order they are loaded in. As each module's dependencies are injected, the module can be tested easily with mocks. RequireJS also keeps all the objects it loads out of the global scope, which decreases the likelihood of namespace collisions in addition to being considered a good general practice.

By default, RequireJS will asynchronously load all of your scripts on demand at runtime. In some cases, this lazy loading is beneficial, but in production, you will want your code bundled into a single file most of the time. RequireJS provides **r.js**, its optimizer, for this. RequireJS can even combine these techniques by bundling multiple groups of files together and then loading these groups on demand at runtime. The best part is that your code won't have to change, regardless of which mode you work in!

 We won't be covering `r.js`, but if you are developing web applications, it might be worth investigating this (see `http://requirejs.org/docs/optimization.html`).

## Asynchronous Module Definitions

**Asynchronous Module Definitions (AMD)** is an important concept in RequireJS: it declares a function whose return value represents the module. In form, it isn't too different from the **Immediately Evaluating Function Expressions (IEFE)** we saw in *Chapter 1, Knockout Essentials*. This is a typical module definition:

```
define('moduleName', ['pathto/dependency'], dependency'],
  function(injectedModule) {
  return //Some module code;
});
```

The `define` method forms the first and only top-level statement in the file. RequireJS actually enforces a one-module-per-file limit by ignoring multiple calls to `define`. The `define` call takes the following three parameters, and the first two are optional:

- **Module name**: This parameter is often ignored, as the standard way to reference modules is by their path. Hence, we will not use this parameter.

- **Dependencies**: This is an array of module names or paths that the module depends on. Paths do not require the `.js` suffix; RequireJS already knows it's loading JavaScript.

- **Module function**: This function receives each dependency from the previous array as a parameter and should return the module.

When RequireJS tries to load a module, it locates the module by path or name and runs the `define` method it finds in that file. First, it checks whether all of the dependencies have been loaded; if they have not been loaded, it recursively loads them, asynchronously and in parallel. When all dependent modules are loaded, it runs the module function, passing in each dependency as a parameter in the same order in which they were declared as dependencies. The return value of the module-loading function is the value that is passed as a parameter to any modules that require it as a dependency.

# Starting RequireJS

There are actually multiple ways to start an app using RequireJS, but by far, the most common way is with a `script` tag that points to the initial script of your application:

```
<script type="text/javascript" src="/lib/require-2.1.js" data-
    main="/app/main"></script>
```

The `data-main` attribute indicates which script will configure RequireJS and start the application. Note that the `.js` suffix is not necessary, as with normal module paths.

This `script` tag typically goes in your shell (or layout) file, and it replaces all of the `script` tags that RequireJS is responsible for loading. In many cases, this means that the only JavaScript `script` tag is the one that loads RequireJS. This is one of the killer features of RequireJS: as we develop, we no longer need to add `script` tags to our HTML code.

Note that the path starts with a forward slash, which makes it an absolute path. It's required because the shell is used on multiple pages, and a relative path will not work on a URL such as `/contacts/1`, as it will look in `/contacts/app/main.js` for our script.

# Configuration

The `main.js` file (the conventional name for the entry point of an AMD application) typically contains a configuration section before the start. Here is the configuration that we will be using:

```
require.config({
  paths: {
    'knockout': '/lib/knockout-3.2.0',
    'bootstrap': '/lib/bootstrap-3.1.1',
    'jquery': '/lib/jquery-2.1.1.min'
  },
  shim: {
    'bootstrap': {
      deps: ['jquery'],
      exports: '$.fn.popover'
    }
  }
});
```

The `paths` section allows us to map paths to module names for use in the dependency arrays. This is a good practice for all library code so that our application code can use a simple, consistent name. Again, the use of absolute paths is important.

The `shim` section is necessary for loading scripts that depend on globally available objects. In the preceding example, the shim for `bootstrap` declares jQuery as a dependency and indicates that it exports `$.fn.popover`. Normally, you would look for a new namespace such as `$.bootstrap`, but as `bootstrap` doesn't create a single endpoint; we are looking for one of the plugins it adds. Any exported value can be used here; `popover` was just the chosen one.

Many libraries are starting to support being loaded as AMD: they look for RequireJS or other module loaders and use them if they are available. Not all libraries do this, though, and the standard model of JavaScript libraries has always been to just look for dependencies in the global scope. As `bootstrap` needs `jQuery` but does not indicate this dependency to RequireJS, it will fail if we tried to load it normally. The shim tells RequireJS that this library is an old global-scope style script and manually indicates its dependencies. The `exports` section provides an object that RequireJS can look for to check whether the script has finished loading. RequireJS will wait until the specified object exists before allowing any AMDs that depend on `bootstrap` to start. Essentially, the `shim` section is how RequireJS uses non-AMD code as an asynchronous dependency. If you need to use jQuery plugins or other non-AMD compatible libraries, just make a shim for them.

There are many other options for the RequireJS configuration—too many to cover here. If you want to learn more, check out their documentation, which is available at `http://requirejs.org/docs/api.html#config`.

# Starting the app

Now that RequireJS is configured, it's time to start the application. The main script, which contains our configuration, is also where RequireJS looks for the initial module, which looks like this:

```
require.config({
  //config
});

define(['jquery', 'knockout', 'contactsPage', 'bootstrap'],
    function($, ko, ContactsPageViewmodel) {
      $(document).ready(function() {
        ko.applyBindings(new ContactsPageViewmodel());
      });
    });
```

The main module is just like other modules, except that RequireJS will run it as soon as its dependencies are available. This code is the same startup code that used to be in the **Contacts** page's script. You might notice that the dependencies for this module don't match the names of the parameters being passed in. jQuery is being injected as `$`, Knockout as `ko`, and the **Contacts** page constructor as `ContactsPageViewModel`. All of these are conventional JavaScript names for their matching objects. The modules are injected in the order of the dependency array; RequireJS doesn't actually look at the name of the parameter. This is no different from standard functions; callers don't care about the names of parameters, they only care about the order. This isn't always obvious to new users, though.

You probably also noticed that `bootstrap` doesn't even have a parameter. This is because `bootstrap` doesn't get its own object; all it does is add functions to jQuery. However, RequireJS won't load it (or shim it, in this case) until a dependency requires it to. It's common to see plugin-style dependencies initialized in this manner, as we want them to be available as soon as the app starts.

To see the `Contacts List` application after it is converted into AMD modules, open the `cp4-contacts` branch. The code was already in IEFE blocks, so not much has changed. The `app` object is no longer required, as namespacing has been replaced with the dependency injection. All of the `script` tags, except for RequireJS, have been removed from the HTML code. The application still functions in the same manner, but by using RequireJS, we no longer have to worry about loading the script. This might seem like a minor gain now, but it will make a big difference when your app starts to grow.

# The text plugin

Managing HTML templates can be tricky, because there is no native way to reference or embed external HTML files like there is with scripts. If you are familiar with the Knockout community, you might have encountered some of the plugins designed to solve the problem, such as *Knockout-External-Templates* (which has been discontinued). RequireJS solves this problem cleanly with the text plugin. The text plugin works much like standard modules: you declare a dependency on external text, and RequireJS injects it into the module just like a normal JavaScript module.

To get started, you should add the text library to your RequireJS config. Using a name such as `text` is standard:

```
require.config({
  paths: {
    'text': '/lib/require-text-2.0.12',
    'knockout': '/lib/knockout-3.2.0',
    'bootstrap': '/lib/bootstrap-3.1.1',
    'jquery': '/lib/jquery-2.1.1.min'
  }
});
```

Once the text plugin is available, you can use it in external files like this:

```
define(['text!some.html'], function (htmlString) {

});
```

This configuration part is optional if the text plugin is at the root of your app and you use the `text!` prefix for dependencies. As we have been putting our third-party libraries in a different folder, the configuration is necessary.

In the next section, we will look at how to combine this ability with components in order to create reusable templates with external, isolated HTML views.

# Components

In Version 3.2, Knockout added components using the combination of a template (view) with a viewmodel to create reusable, behavior-driven DOM objects. Knockout components are inspired by web components, a new (and experimental, at the time of writing this) set of standards that allow developers to define custom HTML elements paired with JavaScript that create packed controls. Like web components, Knockout allows the developer to use custom HTML tags to represent these components in the DOM. Knockout also allows components to be instantiated with a binding handler on standard HTML elements. Knockout binds components by injecting an HTML template, which is bound to its own viewmodel.

This is probably the single largest feature Knockout has ever added to the core library. The reason we started with RequireJS is that components can optionally be loaded and defined with module loaders, including their HTML templates! This means that our entire application (even the HTML) can be defined in independent modules, instead of as a single hierarchy, and loaded asynchronously.

# The basic component registration

Unlike extenders and binding handlers, which are created by just adding an object to Knockout, components are created by calling the `ko.components.register` function:

```
ko.components.register('contact-list, {
  viewModel: function(params) { },
  template: //template string or object
});
```

This will create a new component named `contact-list`, which uses the object returned by the `viewModel` function as a binding context, and the template as its view. It is recommended that you use lowercase, dash-separated names for components so that they can easily be used as custom elements in your HTML.

To use this newly created component, you can use a custom element or the component binding. All the following three tags produce equivalent results:

```
<contact-list params="data: contacts"><contact-list>
<div data-bind="component: { name: 'contact-list', params: { data:
  contacts }"></div>
<!-- ko component: { name: 'contact-list', params: { data:
  contacts } --><!-- /ko -->
```

Obviously, the custom element syntax is much cleaner and easier to read. It is important to note that custom elements cannot be self-closing tags. This is a restriction of the HTML parser and *cannot* be controlled by Knockout.

There is one advantage of using the component binding: the name of the component can be an observable. If the name of the component changes, the previous component will be disposed (just like it would if a control flow binding removed it) and the new component will be initialized.

The `params` attribute of custom elements work in a manner that is similar to the `data-bind` attribute. Comma-separated key/value pairs are parsed to create a property bag, which is given to the component. The values can contain JavaScript literals, observable properties, or expressions. It is also possible to register a component without a viewmodel, in which case, the object created by `params` is directly used as the binding context.

To see this, we'll convert the list of contacts into a component:

```
<contact-list params="contacts: displayContacts,
  edit: editContact,
  delete: deleteContact">
</contact-list>
```

The HTML code for the list is replaced with a custom element with parameters for the list as well as callbacks for the two buttons, which are `edit` and `delete`:

```
ko.components.register('contact-list', {
  template:
  '<ul class="list-unstyled" data-bind="foreach: contacts">'
    +'<li>'
      +'<h3>'
        +'<span data-bind="text: displayName"></span> <small data-
          bind="text: phoneNumber"></small> '
        +'<button class="btn btn-sm btn-default" data-bind="click:
          $parent.edit">Edit</button> '
        +'<button class="btn btn-sm btn-danger" data-bind="click:
          $parent.delete">Delete</button>'
      +'</h3>'
    +'</li>'
  +'</ul>'
});
```

This component registration uses an inline template. You can see this component in the `cp4-inline-component` branch. Everything still looks and works the same, but the resulting HTML now includes our custom element.

```
        <h2>Contacts</h2>
      ► <div class="row">...</div>
      ▼ <contact-list params="contacts: displayContacts, edit: editContact, delete: deleteContact">
         ▼ <ul class="list-unstyled" data-bind="foreach: contacts">
           ► <li>...</li>
           ► <li>...</li>
           ► <li>...</li>
           </ul>
        </contact-list>
      </div>
```

# Custom elements in IE 8 and higher

IE 9 and later versions as well as all other major browsers have no issue with seeing custom elements in the DOM before they have been registered. However, older versions of IE will remove the element if it hasn't been registered. The registration can be done either with Knockout, with `ko.components.register('component-name')`, or with the standard `document.createElement('component-name')` expression statement. One of these must come before the custom element, either by the script containing them being first in the DOM, or by the custom element being added at runtime.

When using RequireJS, being in the DOM first won't help as the loading is asynchronous. If you need to support older IE versions, it is recommended that you include a separate script to register the custom element names at the top of the `body` tag or in the `head` tag:

```html
<!DOCTYPE html>
<html>
  <body>
    <script>
      document.createElement('my-custom-element');
    </script>
    <script src='require.js' data-main='app/startup'></script>

    <my-custom-element></my-custom-element>
  </body>
</html>
```

Once this has been done, components will work in IE 6 and higher even with custom elements.

# Template registration

The `template` property of the configuration sent to register can take any of the following formats:

```js
ko.components.register('component-name', {
  template: [OPTION]
});
```

# The element ID

Consider the following code statement:

```
template: { element: 'component-template' }
```

If you specify the ID of an element in the DOM, the contents of that element will be used as the template for the component. Although it isn't supported in IE yet, the template element is a good candidate, as browsers do not visually render the contents of template elements.

This method can be seen in the cp4-component-id branch.

# The element instance

Consider the following code statement:

```
template: { element: instance }
```

You can pass a real DOM element to the template to be used. This might be useful in a scenario where the template was constructed programmatically. Like the element ID method, only the contents of the elements will be used as the template:

```
var template = document.getElementById('contact-list-template');
ko.components.register('contact-list', {
  template: { element: template }
});
```

This method can be seen in the cp4-component-instance branch.

# An array of DOM nodes

Consider the following code statement:

```
template: [nodes]
```

If you pass an array of DOM nodes to the template configuration, then the entire array will be used as a template and not just the descendants:

```
var template = document.getElementById('contact-list-template')
nodes = Array.prototype.slice.call(template.content.childNodes);
ko.components.register('contact-list', {
  template: nodes
});
```

This can be seen in the cp4-component-arrray branch.

# Document fragments

Consider the following code statement:

```
template: documentFragmentInstance
```

If you pass a document fragment, the entire fragment will be used as a template instead of just the descendants:

```
var template = document.getElementById('contact-list-template');
ko.components.register('contact-list', {
  template: template.content
});
```

This example works because template elements wrap their contents in a document fragment in order to stop the normal rendering. Using the content is the same method that Knockout uses internally when a template element is supplied. This example can be seen in the `cp4-component-fragment` branch.

# HTML strings

We already saw an example for HTML strings in the previous section. While using the value inline is probably uncommon, supplying a string would be an easy thing to do if your build system provided it for you.

# Registering templates using the AMD module

Consider the following code statement:

```
template: { require: 'module/path' }
```

If a `require` property is passed to the configuration object of a template, the default module loader will load the module and use it as the template. The module can return any of the preceding formats. This is especially useful for the RequireJS text plugin:

```
ko.components.register('contact-list', {
  template: { require: 'text!contact-list.html'}
});
```

Using this method, we can extract the HTML template into its own file, drastically improving its organization. By itself, this is a huge benefit to development. An example of this can be seen in the `cp4-component-text` branch.

# The viewmodel registration

Like template registration, viewmodels can be registered using several different formats. To demonstrate this, we'll use a simple viewmodel of our contacts list components:

```
function ListViewmodel(params) {
  this.contacts = params.contacts;
  this.edit = params.edit;
  this.delete = function(contact) {
    console.log('Mock Deleting Contact', ko.toJS(contact));
  };
};
```

To verify that things are getting wired up properly, you'll want something interactive; hence, we use the fake `delete` function.

## The constructor function

Consider the following code statement:

```
viewModel: Constructor
```

If you supply a function to the `viewModel` property, it will be treated as a constructor. When the component is instantiated, `new` will be called on the function, with the `params` object as its first parameter:

```
ko.components.register('contact-list', {
  template: { require: 'text!contact-list.html'},
  viewModel: ListViewmodel //Defined above
});
```

This method can be seen in the `cp4-components-constructor` branch.

## A singleton object

Consider the following code statement:

```
viewModel: { instance: singleton }
```

If you want all your component instances to be backed by a shared object—though this is not recommended—you can pass it as the `instance` property of a configuration object. Because the object is shared, parameters cannot be passed to the viewmodel using this method.

# The factory function

Consider the following code statement:

```
viewModel: { createViewModel: function(params, componentInfo) {} }
```

This method is useful because it supplies the container element of the component to the second parameter on `componentInfo.element`. It also provides you with the opportunity to perform any other setup, such as modifying or extending the constructor parameters. The `createViewModel` function should return an instance of a viewmodel component:

```
ko.components.register('contact-list', {
  template: { require: 'text!contact-list.html'},
  viewModel: { createViewModel: function(params, componentInfo) {
    console.log('Initializing component for',
      componentInfo.element);
    return new ListViewmodel(params);
  }}
});
```

This example can be seen in the `cp4-component-factory` branch.

# Registering viewmodels using an AMD module

Consider the following code statement:

```
viewModel: { require: 'module-path' }
```

Just like templates, viewmodels can be registered with an AMD module that returns any of the preceding formats.

In the `cp4-component-module` branch, you can see an example of this. The component registration has been moved to the `main.js` file.

# Registering AMD

In addition to registering the template and the viewmodel as AMD modules individually, you can register the entire component with a require call:

```
ko.components.register('contact-list', { require: 'contact-list'
  });
```

The AMD module will return the entire component configuration:

```
define(['knockout', 'text!contact-list.html'], function(ko,
  templateString) {
```

```
function ListViewmodel(params) {
  this.contacts = params.contacts;
  this.edit = params.edit;
  this.delete = function(contact) {
    console.log('Mock Deleting Contact', ko.toJS(contact));
  };
}

return { template: templateString, viewModel: ListViewmodel };
});
```

As the Knockout documentation points out, this method has several benefits:

- The registration call is just a `require` path, which is easy to manage.
- The component is composed of two parts: a JavaScript module and an HTML module. This provides both simple organization and clean separation.
- The RequireJS optimizer, which is `r.js`, can use the text dependency on the HTML module to bundle the HTML code with the bundled output. This means your entire application, including the HTML templates, can be a single file in production (or a collection of bundles if you want to take advantage of lazy loading).

You can see an example of this in the `cp4-component-amd` branch. This is the recommended pattern for components and is the one that will be used for the rest of the examples in this chapter.

# Observing changes in component parameters

Component parameters will be passed via the `params` object to the component's viewmodel in one of the following three ways:

- No observable expression evaluation needs to occur, and the value is passed literally:

```
<component params="name: 'Timothy Moran'"></component>
<component params="name: nonObservableProperty">
  </component>
<component params="name: observableProperty"></component>
<component params="name: viewModel.observableSubProperty
  "></component>
```

  In all of these cases, the value is passed directly to the component on the `params` object. This means that changes to these values will change the property on the instantiating viewmodel, except for the first case (literal values). Observable values can be subscribed to normally.

- An observable expression needs to be evaluated, so it is wrapped in a computed observable:

```
<component params="name: name() + '!'"></component>
```

In this case, `params.name` is not the original property. Calling `params.name()` will evaluate the computed wrapper. Trying to modify the value will fail, as the computed value is not writable. The value can be subscribed to normally.

- An observable expression evaluates an observable instance, so it is wrapped in an observable that unwraps the result of the expression:

```
<component params="name: isFormal() ? firstName :
  lastName"></component>
```

In this example, `firstName` and `lastName` are both observable properties. If calling `params.name()` returned the observable, you will need to call `params.name()()` to get the actual value, which is rather ugly. Instead, Knockout automatically unwraps the expression so that calling `params.name()` returns the actual value of either `firstName` or `lastName`.

If you need to access the actual observable instances to, for example, write a value to them, trying to write to `params.name` will fail, as it is a computed observable. To get the unwrapped value, you can use the `params.$raw` object, which provides the unwrapped values. In this case, you can update the name by calling `params.$raw.name('New')`.

In general, this case should be avoided by removing the logic from the binding expression and placing it in a computed observable in the viewmodel.

# The component's life cycle

When a component binding is applied, Knockout takes the following steps.

1. The component loader asynchronously creates the viewmodel factory and template. This result is cached so that it is only performed once per component.
2. The template is cloned and injected into the container (either the custom element or the element with the component binding).
3. If the component has a viewmodel, it is instantiated. This is done synchronously.
4. The component is bound to either the viewmodel or the `params` object.
5. The component is left *active* until it is disposed.
6. The component is disposed. If the viewmodel has a `dispose` method, it is called, and then the template is removed from the DOM.

# The component's disposal

If the component is removed from the DOM by Knockout, either because of the name of the component binding or a control flow binding being changed (for example, `if` and `foreach`), the component will be disposed. If the component's viewmodel has a `dispose` function, it will be called. Normal Knockout bindings in the components view will be automatically disposed, just as they would in a normal control flow situation. However, anything set up by the viewmodel needs to be manually cleaned up. Some examples of viewmodel cleanup include the following:

- The `setInterval` callbacks can be removed with `clearInterval`.
- Computed observables can be removed by calling their `dispose` method. Pure computed observables don't need to be disposed. Computed observables that are only used by bindings or other viewmodel properties also do not need to be disposed, as garbage collection will catch them.
- Observable subscriptions can be disposed by calling their `dispose` method.
- Event handlers can be created by components that are not part of a normal Knockout binding.

You can see a simple dispose handler in the `cp4-dispose` branch. It just logs to the console to demonstrate when it will fire; try editing a contact to make the control flow remove the list from the page.

# Combining components with data bindings

There is only one restriction of `data-bind` attributes that are used on custom elements with the component binding: the binding handlers cannot use `controlsDescendantBindings`. This isn't a new restriction; two bindings that control descendants cannot be on a single element, and since components control descendant bindings that cannot be combined with a binding handler that also controls descendants. It is worth remembering, though, as you might be inclined to place an `if` or `foreach` binding on a component; doing this will cause an error. Instead, wrap the component with an element or a containerless binding:

```
<ul data-bind='foreach: allProducts'>
  <product-details params='product: $data'></product-details>
</ul>
```

It's also worth noting that bindings such as `text` and `html` will replace the contents of the element they are on. When used with components, this will potentially result in the component being lost, so it's not a good idea.

# Custom component loaders

So far, we have covered the behavior of the default component loader. It is quite flexible, and for many developers, it will be quite sufficient for most use cases. However, it is possible to implement the custom component-loading functionality. In fact, you can have multiple component loaders active simultaneously, each providing different capabilities.

This section will deal with creating custom component loaders. If you are satisfied with the functionality of the default loader, you might want to skip this section and continue to single page application routing.

First, let's cover how the component-loading system works. Component loading is only done once per component. Knockout caches the loaded components. This cache provides the following two public functions:

- `ko.components.get(name, callback)`: This function loops through all the loaders until one of them returns a component. This component is cached, and then the callback is invoked with it.
- `ko.components.clearCachedDefinition(name)`: This function removes the component from the registry.

Knockout maintains an array of loaders on `ko.components.loaders`. By default, this array only contains a single loader, which also lives on `ko.components.defaultLoader`. When a component binding requests a component, or you call `ko.components.get`, Knockout loops through the loaders, calling `getConfig` on each component until it gets a non-null object. This configuration is then passed to each loader until a valid component object is returned. The loaded component is then cached. A valid component object has the following properties:

- `template`: This is an array of DOM nodes
- `createViewModel(params, componentInfo)`: This is an optional factory method to build components

# Implementing a component loader

All of the methods are optional on a component loader, as Knockout will run through each method on each loader until it gets a valid response before repeating it on the next method. All component loader functions are asynchronous by supplying a callback. Remember, the result will be cached unless manually cleared with `ko.components.clearCachedDefinition(componentName)`. The following are the methods used to implement a component loader:

- `getConfig(name, callback)`: This returns a component configuration object. A configuration object is anything that any loader's `loadComponent` function can understand.

- `loadComponent(name, componentConfig, callback)`: This supplies a component object of the `{ template: domNodeArray, createViewModel(params, componentInfo) }` type.

- `loadTemplate(name, templateConfig, callback)`: This supplies an array of DOM nodes to be used as the template.

- `loadViewModel(name, viewModelConfig, callback)`: This supplies a function to be used as the `createViewModel(params, componentInfo)` factory.

To implement a method, just include it in your loader. To have your loader skip a method that it has implemented, call `callback(null)`.

The last two methods are not directly called by the Knockout component system but by the default loader's `loadComponent` method.

# The default loader

To understand how the methods on a custom loader can be made optional, you must understand how the default loader works. The default loader has an internal registry for component configurations—not to be confused with the cache for components. The default loader adds the following methods to the `ko.components` object in order to work with the component configuration registry:

- `ko.components.register(name, configuration)`: This is covered in the previous section in detail

- `ko.components.isRegistered(name)`: This returns `true` if the component configuration is in the registry; otherwise, it returns `false`

- `ko.unregister(name)`: This removes the named configuration if it exists

When Knockout tries to load a component for the first time, it calls `getConfig` on each loader in `ko.components.loaders` until one returns a non-null object. Then, it passes that configuration object to `loadComponent` on each loader until one returns a non-null component object. If a loader other than the default loader returns a component from `loadComponent`, the chain ends there.

However, the default loader's `loadComponent` method calls `loadTemplate` and `loadViewModel` on each loader (including itself) until it gets both a template and a viewmodel. These calls are independent; the default loader will take the first template it gets and the first viewmodel it gets even if they are from different loaders. If your custom loader has a higher priority than the default loader, or if the default loader can't understand your configuration, your custom loader will have a chance to supply its own template and/or viewmodel by implementing `loadTemplate` or `loadViewModel`.

# Registering a custom loader

Unlike `ko.bindingHandlers` and `ko.extenders`, which are both objects, `ko.components.loaders` is an array. Once you have created your custom loader, you can add it to the `loaders` array. The order of the `loaders` array determines the priority; Knockout always loops through the loaders from the first to the last:

- For a lower priority custom loader, use `ko.components.loaders.push(loader)`

- For a higher priority custom loader, use `ko.components.loaders.unshift(loader)`

- For a fine-grained control custom loader, use `ko.components.loaders.splice(priority, 0, loader)`, where priority is the 0-index rank of the new loader

If you remove the default loader from `ko.component.loaders`, then `loadTemplate` and `loadViewModel` will no longer be called (unless they are called by another custom loader). As it is possible to simply add a custom loader with a higher priority, there is little value in removing the default loader.

# Registering custom elements

Custom elements work in Knockout by wrapping the component binding. There are two options that can be used to get Knockout to treat a custom element as a component:

- Call `ko.components.register('component-name', { /* config */ }.`

- Override `ko.components.getComponentNameForNode(node)` so that it returns the name of a component. Components do not need to be registered as long as a loader that can load the name returned by this method exists. The default loader will only load components registered with `ko.components.register`.

# Loading components with custom configurations

Alright, it's time to look at an example. This one is taken from the Knockout component's documentation. Let's say you are using our own asynchronous loading library for the HTML, and you want your custom loader to use it. This could be true for a JavaScript loader, which the documentation provides as an example, but it would be similar enough to be redundant here. It will use its own configuration property name in order to avoid confusion with the default loader:

```
ko.components.register('contact-list', {
  template: { fromUrl: 'contact-list.html', maxCacheAge: 100 },
  viewModel: { require: 'contact-list'  }
});
```

As the default loader will pass this configuration to the `loadTemplate` method of each loader, we can just implement that one method:

```
var templateFromUrlLoader = {
  loadTemplate: function(name, templateConfig, callback) {
    if (templateConfig.fromUrl) {
      // Uses jQuery's ajax facility to load the markup from a
        file
      var fullUrl = '/app/' + templateConfig.fromUrl +
        '?cacheAge=' + templateConfig.maxCacheAge;
      $.get(fullUrl, function(markupString) {
        callback($.parseHTML(markupString));
      });
    } else {
      // Unrecognized config format. Let another loader handle it.
      callback(null);
    }
  }
};
```

This loader will use jQuery to retrieve and parse the template if it has the `fromUrl` property; otherwise, it will do nothing. The only thing that's left is to add the loader to Knockout:

```
ko.components.loaders.unshift(templateFromUrlLoader);
```

You can see this custom loader in the `cp4-loader` branch; it is in the `main.js` file.

Knockout's default component loader is already flexible, but the ability to provide your own custom loader for both configuration and instantiation gives the Knockout component system the ability to work with whichever format you want to create.

# Single Page Application (SPA) routing

A big part of the appeal of Knockout (or any MV* framework) is that its template engine allows us to rerender parts of the page without the need to talk to the server. Being able to make incremental page updates on the client side means less latency, giving the application a much snappier feel. SPAs take this concept to the next level by letting the JavaScript client control navigation between pages. When the browser navigates, it has to rerender the whole page, which means reloading the JavaScript, HTML, CSS, and everything. When JavaScript *navigates*, it just has to change part of the HTML, which ends up being much faster in most cases.

Knockout can provide this virtual page-changing functionality relatively easily, but an important component of SPAs is that page changes still update the URL. This helps the user check whether a change has occurred, but more importantly, it means that if the user refreshes the page or shares the link, the application will go to the right page. Without the URL update, the user will always end up on the home screen. This feature is commonly known as **routing**. Knockout does not provide this mechanism.

To explore how Knockout fits into an SPA scenario, we are going to use SammyJS (`http://sammyjs.org/`). SammyJS is a popular library used for routing; Knockout even uses it on its tutorial site. There are many other options, of course, but the concept should be very similar regardless of which library you use.

# An overview of SammyJS

SammyJS's default routing uses hash-change navigation, which uses the URL hash to store the current state. As the hash is not sent to the server by the browser, the server always sees the URL as a request for the home page. Once the page loads, Sammy will inspect the hash and locate the matching route, if one exists. If it finds a route, it runs the callback for that route. The callback is responsible for performing whatever application logic is necessary for navigation. The following code demonstrates this:

```
var app = Sammy('#appHost', function() {
  //Home route
    this.get('#/', function() {
    //Load home page
  });
    this.get('#/contacts/:id', function() {
      var contactId = this.params.id;
      //Load contact
    });
}).run('#/');
```

This is a typical Sammy application configuration. The `Sammy` object is a function that takes an element's ID, which it will scope the handler to, and an initialization handler and returns the application object. Inside the initialization handler, this has methods for each HTTP verb that registers routes. The preceding sample registers a route for #/ (a standard *home* route) and a route for #/contacts/:id. The :id part of the route indicates a parameter that will match any contents and provide the value on the `params` object inside the route's callback.

The application object that is returned from `Sammy()` will not start until `run()` is called, which should wait for the DOM to be ready. The `run()` method takes a default route, which will be loaded if no hash is present (such as when navigating to the bare domain URL).

# Controlling the navigation

SammyJS monitors the `window.location.hash` property for any changes and runs the matching route handler. This can happen when a user clicks on an a tag with an `href` attribute containing a hash or by setting `window.location.hash` from JavaScript. Using the window object inside viewmodels is generally discouraged, as it is difficult to mock in unit tests. It would also be nice to keep the navigation logic centralized, just in case it needs to be changed later. To do this, we will encapsulate the navigation into a router module. For now, it only needs a single method:

```
define(function() {
    return {
```

```
    navigate: function(path) {
      window.location.hash = '#' + path;
    }
  };
});
```

Once injected with RequireJS, viewmodels can be navigated by calling `router.navigate`.

# Creating page components

There are a lot of different ways to organize Knockout viewmodels in SPAs and web apps in general. As we just learned how to create components, we are going to look at a method used to structure each page as a component. This gives us a few solid advantages:

- The pages will be decoupled from each other
- Each page will have its own HTML and JavaScript file, which feels natural
- A single component binding on the shell can hold the *body* of the page while maintaining a static layout for the navigation bar

At some point, we will need to introduce a folder structure that will keep these files organized, so we might as well start now.

The home page (which was just a greeting) has been removed, but the placeholder settings page is still there so that we have at least two links to test navigation with. The router and mock data service have been moved into the `core` folder (a name I prefer because it's shorter than `common`). The rest of the code, which consists of the contact model and the two pages, has been moved into the `contacts` folder. The `main.js` starting file hasn't moved.

You can, of course, group files whichever way you want; nothing we have covered so far will require any specific file structure.

## The edit page

Previously, both pages were managed by a single viewmodel that switched between them using a null *editing* contact. However, it was clear that this combined viewmodel was serving multiple roles. Splitting the editing code should reduce some confusion:

```javascript
define(['knockout', 'text!contacts/edit.html', 'core/dataService',
    'core/router', 'contacts/contact'],
function(ko, templateString, dataService, router, Contact) {

    function ContactEditViewmodel(params) {
        self.entryContact = ko.observable(new Contact());
        if (params && params.id) {
            dataService.getContact(params.id, function(contact) {
                if (contact)
                    self.entryContact(contact);
            });
        }

        self.cancelEntry = function() {
            router.navigate('/');
        };
        self.saveEntry = function() {

            var action = self.entryContact().id() === 0
            ? dataService.createContact
            : dataService.updateContact;

            action(self.entryContact(), function() {
                router.navigate('/');
            });
        };
        self.dispose = function() {
            self.entryContact(null);
```

```
    };
  }

  return {
    template: templateString,
    viewModel: ContactEditViewmodel
  };
});
```

There are only three real changes here:

- First, instead of clearing the entryContact object to indicate that editing is finished, the viewmodel calls router.navigate('/'). As we don't have a home page anymore, the list page will be used as the default page, which will be tied to the / route.

- Secondly, as editing will occur based on navigation instead of the entryContact object being set directly, the viewmodel uses the params component to look for an ID. If an ID isn't present, it is assumed that we are creating a new contact; if an ID is present, the contact is loaded from the data service.

- Finally, a dispose method has been added, which will clear the entryContact object. This isn't actually necessary, but it demonstrates how the clean up will be done.

The HTML code hasn't really changed, except that it will be in its own file now.

# The list page

The list page will be the new home page. Like the edit page, it will need to use the router to navigate to the edit page instead of using the entryContact object. The list page doesn't need any parameters:

```
define(['knockout', 'text!contacts/list.html', 'core/dataService',
  'core/router'],
function(ko, templateString, dataService, router) {

  function ContactsListViewmodel() {
    var self = this;

    self.contacts = ko.observableArray();

    dataService.getContacts(function(contacts) {
      self.contacts(contacts);
    });
```

```
    self.newEntry = function() { router.navigate('/contacts/new');
      };
    self.editContact = function(contact) {
      router.navigate('/contacts/' + contact.id()); };

    self.deleteContact = function(contact) {
      dataService.removeContact(contact.id(), function() {
        self.contacts.remove(contact);
        });
    };

    self.query = ko.observable('');
    self.clearQuery = function() { self.query(''); };

    self.displayContacts = ko.computed(function() {
      //Same as before
    });

    self.dispose = function() {
      self.contacts.removeAll();
    };
  }

  return {
    template: templateString,
    viewModel: ContactsListViewmodel
  };
});
```

Here too, the HTML code hasn't changed much, except that the `contact-list` component has been removed, so its view has been re-added to the list page.

# Coordinating pages

So far, the example server has been responsible for putting each page into our shell/ layout HTML by performing a string replace. To get the experience of a real SPA, we are going to change the server to return an index file without performing any parsing or rendering on it:

```
<!DOCTYPE html>
<html>
  <head>
    //Same as before
  </head>
```

```
<body>
  <!-- Navbar -->
  <nav class="navbar navbar-default" role="navigation">
    //Same as before
  </nav>

  <!-- Main Application Body -->
  <div id="appHost" class="container" data-bind="if: name">
    <!-- ko component: { name: name, params: data } --><!-- /ko
      -->
  </div>
  <script type="text/javascript" src="/lib/require-2.1.js" data-
    main="/app/main"></script>
</body>
</html>
```

The `appHost` element in the preceding code contains a containerless component binding that uses an observable `name` and `params` value. It's wrapped in an `if` binding that ensures that the component binding isn't active until a page has been selected. All the root viewmodel has to do is supply the `name` and `params` properties.

For this, our `main.js` will contain a simple viewmodel that contains each property. The SammyJS route handlers will set this viewmodel when the routes are activated. The `main.js` file will also be responsible for registering the page components with Knockout. It's long, so we are going to break it up into chunks:

```
define(['jquery', 'knockout', 'sammy', 'bootstrap'], function($,
  ko, Sammy) {
  var pageVm = {
    name: ko.observable(),
    data: ko.observable(),
    setRoute: function(name, data) {
      //Set data first, otherwise component will get old data
      this.data(data);
      this.name(name);
    }
  };

  //Sammy Setup
  Var sammyConfig = /* see below */

  $(document).ready(function() {
    sammyConfig.run('#/');
    ko.applyBindings(pageVm);
  });
});
```

SammyJS has been added as a dependency and injected in. The RequireJS configuration isn't shown, but it doesn't require a shim. SammyJS plays nicely as an AMD. The `pageVm` object is created with two observable properties and a helper method for setting them. The order is important because component viewmodels are instantiated synchronously, and the data bound to the `params` object needs to already be in place when the component name changes; otherwise, the component will initialize before the `params` objects are set.

After SammyJS has been set up, the document-ready handler starts it using a default route and then applies bindings with the `pageVm` object.

One way to perform the SammyJS configuration would be to write out each component register and route handler, as follows:

```
ko.components.register('contact-edit', { require: 'contacts/edit'
  });
self.get('#/contacts/:id', function() {
  pageVm.setRoute('contact-edit', { id: this.params.id });
});
```

Personally, I think this ends up being a bit messy. It also duplicates the component name in `register` and `setRoute`. SammyJS also doesn't allow you to bind multiple routes to the same handler in a single call; you have to write both of them out. This is especially annoying for the home page, because SammyJS treats an empty route and the #/ route as different routes, even though they both conventionally mean *home*. To solve these, we can combine the component and route definitions into a page object, and then loop over them:

```
var sammyConfig = Sammy('#appHost', function() {
  var self = this;
  var pages = [
    { route: ['/', '#/'], component: 'contact-list',     module:
      'contacts/list'}, { route: ['#/contacts/new',
      '#/contacts/:id'], component: 'contact-edit',     module:
      'contacts/edit' }, { route: '#/settings', component:
      'settings-page', module: 'settings/page' }
  ];

  pages.forEach(function(page) {
    //Register the component, only needs to happen
    ko.components.register(page.component, { require: page.module
      });

    //Force routes to be an array
    if (!(page.route instanceof Array))
```

```
      page.route = [page.route];

   //Register routes with Sammy
   page.route.forEach(function(route) {
     self.get(route, function() {

       //Collect the parameters, if present
       var params = {};
       ko.utils.objectForEach(this.params, function(name, value)
         {
         params[name] = value;
       });

       //Set the page
       pageVm.setRoute(page.component, params);
     });
   });
 });
});
```

Much better. Now, it's easy to see how the routes and components are related, and defining multiple routes for a single component is simple. It also removes the duplicated component name.

The `instanceof` check lets us use an array or a string for the `page.route` property by always making it an array. The `params` section will include any parameters captured by the route handler and will pass them as the data used by the component binding for the `params` object.

All the code we just covered can be seen in the `cp4-spa` branch. Be sure to use each page on the app, and notice the URL change. If you go to a page, such as a specific contact, and refresh the browser, SammyJS will make sure that the correct page is loaded instead of always going to the home page. This gives the application a very natural feel. You should also notice that moving between pages happens with little or no delay (depending on your CPU). For comparison, try to view changes between the `/contacts` and `/settings` pages in the `cp4-contacts` branch. The SPA navigation is much faster.

# Summary

By now, you should have a good idea or two about how to structure a Knockout web application, specifically, a single page application. The Knockout components feature gives you a powerful tool that will help you create reusable, behavior-driven DOM elements, and writing custom loaders allows you to fully control how components are used. The RequireJS AMD patterns make application organization easy by splitting up JavaScript and HTML into independent modules. Because these modules use dependency injection, creating mocks for unit testing is also possible. Finally, you saw how SammyJS can create fast client-side JavaScript navigation with pages controlled by components.

In the next chapter, we will look at the Durandal framework, which will make the single page application development even easier.

# 5
# Durandal – the Knockout Framework

In the previous chapter, we looked at how to use RequireJS and SammyJS with Knockout, to add more standard functionality to our frontend stack with module definitions and client-side routing. Both of these concepts have become very common in the JavaScript world; you might even consider them as a standard for modern web applications. Knockout is a library and not a framework, in that it fills a specific role—data-binding—instead of trying to be the entire development framework for the frontend. This leaves a lot of decisions to be made if you want to create a modern JavaScript client, which can be burdensome, time-consuming, and, if your team is divided, contentious. Durandal is a framework that attempts to make many of these decisions while still keeping Knockout's MVVM philosophy in mind.

Durandal was created by Blue Spire, whose principal developer, Rob Eisenberg, also created the popular WPF framework Caliburn.Micro, another MVVM framework. Over the next two chapters, we will be looking at how Durandal can help us build web applications easily while leveraging all of our experience and custom code from Knockout. This chapter is going to cover the following:

- Overview of the Durandal framework
- The composition system
- The router
- Modal dialogs
- The application's life cycle
- Widgets

Once again, we will be using the Contacts application with the chapter's examples.

# An overview of the Durandal framework

Durandal is built on top of Knockout, jQuery, and RequireJS. Durandal's core is a collection of AMD modules, which provide composition, events, and activation features, as well as some utility functions. In addition to the core modules, Durandal also provides several plugins that can optionally be activated, or added to with community or personal plugins. The plugins include the router (a basic requirement for every SPA framework), dialogs, and widgets.

 The documentation for Durandal can be found at http://durandaljs.com/docs.html.

# Promises

To bring all of this together, Durandal's internal and external communication is handled through **promises**. If you aren't familiar with JavaScript promises—sometimes called *thenables* because they provide a then method—you're missing out. To explain briefly, promises change the way asynchronous actions are handled by replacing a callback with a return object that represents the asynchronous work. It allows asynchronous tasks to be chained, and does error handling in a simple, easy-to-debug manner. I won't be covering how promises work here, but it is going to be relevant. You should read up on them if you haven't already done so.

If you are familiar with promises, you may already know that jQuery's promise implementation does not match the A+ specification (https://promisesaplus.com), which most other promise libraries conform to. To minimize third-party dependencies, Durandal uses jQuery's promises by default, but their documentation provides a simple patch to allow the use of another promise implementation. This example, which uses Q (a very popular promise library), is taken from the Durandal documentation. Use it before the call to app.start() (we will learn more about this later):

```
system.defer = function (action) {
  var deferred = Q.defer();
  action.call(deferred, deferred);
  var promise = deferred.promise;
  deferred.promise = function() {
    return promise;
  };
  return deferred;
};
```

If you prefer another library, simply replace Q in the preceding code. I will be using Durandal's default promises in this chapter for simplicity, but I encourage you to use an A+ compliant implementation in real-world applications.

# Getting started

While Durandal's only real requirement on your filesystem is that all its core modules should be in the same folder and all its plugins should be in their own folder, there are some conventions for the way things are organized, as shown in the following screenshot:

This should be familiar, as it isn't too different from what we have been using. The app directory contains our code, the lib directory contains third-party code, and the content directory contains our CSS and other visual assets. Durandal's entire source, which contains some of its own CSS, its core modules, as well as the standard plugins directory, is dropped into lib. Our main.js configuration looks like this:

```
require.config({
  paths: {
    'text': '../lib/require/text',
    'durandal':'../lib/durandal/js',
    'plugins' : '../lib/durandal/js/plugins',
    'transitions' : '../lib/durandal/js/transitions',
    'knockout': '../lib/knockout-3.1.0',
    'bootstrap': '../lib/bootstrap-3.1.1',
    'jquery': '../lib/jquery-2.1.1.min'
  },
  shim: {
    'bootstrap': {
      deps: ['jquery'],
      exports: 'jQuery'
    }
  },
  waitSeconds: 30
});
```

There shouldn't be anything surprising here, as we covered the configuration of RequireJS in the previous chapter. All of the paths, except `bootstrap`, are required by Durandal. After configuration, Durandal needs to be initialized; this is generally placed in `main.js`, just below `require.config`:

```
define(['durandal/system', 'durandal/app'],
function(system, app, extensions) {

  system.debug(true);

  //specify which plugins to install and their configuration
  app.configurePlugins({
    //Durandal plugins
    router:true,
    dialog: true
  });

  app.title = 'Mastering Knockout';
  app.start().then(function () {
    app.setRoot('shell/shell');
  });
});
```

The `app` and `system` modules are Durandal objects. The `system.debug` call instructs Durandal to log all of the steps it takes to the console, which is useful for development. The `app.configurePlugins` call registers the plugins to be installed, though they are not run until `app.start` is called. The `app.start` call initializes all the Durandal modules and installs the registered plugins. As `app.start` is a promise-returning function, a `then` method is attached, which calls `app.setRoot` when it is finished. The `setRoot` method composes the specified module into the DOM as the root viewmodel of the application.

The root of the application is placed inside a `div` element with the `applicationHost` ID, which is expected to be in the DOM already. As Durandal will take care of all the HTML rendering, the original DOM is pretty thin. It only requires the CSS that will be used, the `applicationHost` ID, and the `script` tag for RequireJS. This is the standard `index.html` file:

```
<!DOCTYPE html>
<html>
  <head>
    <title>Mastering Knockout</title>
    <meta name="viewport" content="width=device-width, initial-
      scale=1.0">
```

```
   <link rel="stylesheet" href="content/css/bootstrap-3.1.1-
      darkly.css" type="text/css" media="all"  title="darkly" />
   <link rel="alternate stylesheet" href="content/css/bootstrap-
      3.1.1-cosmo.css" type="text/css" media="all" title="cosmo"
      />
   <link rel="stylesheet" href="content/css/font-awesome-
      4.0.3.css" type="text/css" media="all" />

   <link rel="stylesheet" href="lib/durandal/css/durandal.css" />
   <link rel="stylesheet" href="content/css/app.css"
</head>
<body>
   <!-- Main Application Body -->
   <div id="applicationHost"></div>
   <script type="text/javascript" src="lib/require/require.js"
      data-main="app/main"></script>
</body>
</html>
```

That's it! Durandal has been started and everything after this point is going to be your application's code.

# The composition system

In the previous chapter, we looked at Knockout's new components feature, which lets us construct view/viewmodel pairs by instantiating them from the DOM with custom elements (or bindings). Knockout released this feature after Durandal, so there is some overlap between the two. Durandal's composition is like a blend of the components and the template binding.

Composition is primarily invoked in two ways, with `setRoot` to compose the `applicationHost` ID, and with the compose binding for data-bound values. Composition works by pairing a viewmodel with a view.

> Durandal's documentation refers to viewmodels as modules, which I think is a bit confusing. I will be referring to composable modules as viewmodels throughout this chapter.

When composition is given a viewmodel, it looks up the view, loads it with the RequireJS's text loader, binds it to the view, and finally, attaches it to the DOM.

# Composing the application's root

Let's look at the root composition of our shell viewmodel. Our preceding sample was setting the root to `shell/shell`. If our `app` directory has a `shell` folder, the `shell.js` module will be loaded by `setRoot` and composed. Composition uses Durandal's `viewLocator` module to find an HTML file, by replacing the file extension of the module; so for `shell.js`, it will look for `shell.html` and use it as the view.

You can see a very simple example of this in `cp5-shell`. The `shell` module is very simple, containing just a `title` property that we will bind to:

```
define(function (ko, app) {
  return {
    title: 'Welcome!'
  };
});
```

The `shell.html` view is a bare HTML snippet. It does not contain the standard `<html>` root element:

```
<div class="jumbotron">
  <h1 data-bind="text: title"></h1>
  <p>This HTML was rendered into the DOM with Durandal's
    composition system. Notice the data-binding on the
    <code>h1</code> tag with the viewmodel property
    <code>title</code>.</p>
</div>
```

Durandal expects views to be partial HTML documents. They should not contain an HTML, HEAD, or BODY element; they should contain only the HTML that will be used as the template for the DOM contents.

If you run the code, you will see that this HTML is rendered into the DOM, and the title is bound to the `shell` module's `title` property. The object returned by the `shell` module is used as the binding context for the shell's view.

# The compose binding

Generally, the root of the application does not change, and instead, serves as the layout or shell for the HTML. It displays content that is present on every page (such as a navigation bar), and hence it doesn't need to change. Composition can also be invoked with the compose binding, which takes a viewmodel as a binding value.

Open the `cp5-composition` branch. Notice that the shell view is back to containing our familiar navigation bar, as well as a compose binding, in its main content area:

```
<div>
  <nav class="…" role="banner">
    //Standard Nav Bar HTML you've seen in every other sample
  </nav>

  <div class="page-host container">
    <div data-bind="compose: currentModel"></div>
  </div>
</div>
```

The shell viewmodel has a `currentModel` property, as well as two functions, to switch the `currentModel` property between the `edit` and `list` page objects:

```
define(['knockout', 'durandal/app', 'contacts/edit',
  'contacts/list'],
function (ko, app, EditVm, ListVm) {
  var listVm = new ListVm(),
  editVm = new EditVm();
  return {
    title: app.title,
    currentModel: ko.observable(listVm),
    setEdit: function() { this.currentModel(editVm); },
    setList: function() { this.currentModel(listVm); }
  };
});
```

Try pressing the buttons in the navigation bar to see the body content switch between the two pages. The compose binding is taking a module instance, locating its view, and binding the view as the content of the DOM. As `currentModel` is observable, the composition reruns anytime it changes.

As the `list` and `edit` objects are constructed once and just swapped, you should notice that values entered on the edit page are persistent. This is because, while the HTML is discarded and recreated when switching, the new HTML is still being bound against the same object.

Hopefully, the brevity of this example doesn't undercut the power of the composition system. The fact that they are so small should highlight just how easy composition is to work with; just by swapping a bound value, we can toggle between two completely different pages!

You may have noticed that composition is like a mirror of Knockout components. Instead of a custom element or binding in the DOM choosing what will be rendered, composition renders the value specified by JavaScript. This ends up having a large impact on flexibility. A component is the element that the DOM says it is, but a single compose binding can hold any module and it can change at any time. They may seem like competing features, but I think they are serving different goals.

Components are like advanced binding handlers, allowing the HTML to instantiate behavior-driven templates.

Composition uses the relationships created and managed by our viewmodel code and reflects them in the presentation layer.

# Composition options

We looked at two examples of composition—`setRoot` and the compose binding—that each took an instance of an object to compose. Of course, Durandal is a thoughtful framework, so the composition has several other modes of operation. The value taken by the compose binding can be any of the following.

## Module instance

We've already covered this, but for the sake of completion, the compose binding can take an instance of a module and use it to locate the view. See the `cp5-composition` branch for an example. This is the most common use case for composition with the compose binding.

## Constructor

In the `cp5-composition2` branch, you can see a modified shell that sets the `currentModel` property to the constructor functions directly:

```
define(['knockout', 'durandal/app', 'contacts/edit',
  'contacts/list'],
function (ko, app, EditVm, ListVm) {
  return {
    title: app.title,
    currentModel: ko.observable(ListVm),
    setEdit: function() { this.currentModel(EditVm); },
   setList: function() { this.currentModel(ListVm); }
  };
});
```

While this isn't a great use case, it is supported. Constructors are most commonly used for modules tied to the router, as a fresh viewmodel is generally desirable when navigating between pages. Unlike the previous example, which stored a reference to a constructed viewmodel for each page, this method will recreate the viewmodel each time it navigates.

## Module ID strings

There are two ways to use strings for the compose binding value. The first is by supplying a module ID. You can see this in the cp5-composition3 branch:

```
currentModel: ko.observable(''contacts/list''),
setEdit: function() { this.currentModel(''contacts/edit''); },
setList: function() { this.currentModel('contacts/list'); }
```

This results in the module being composed. If the module returns an object, it is composed directly; if the module returns a function, it is treated as a constructor to create the object. Of course, because it's a string, this could be used in the binding directly:

```
<div data-bind="compose: 'contacts/list'"></div>
```

While supported, I personally feel like this violates the separation of concerns. It ties the HTML view directly to a viewmodel.

## Viewpath strings

The second way to use strings in the compose binding is with a viewpath. If the string contains an extension that the viewEngine module recognizes, it will be used to load that view and bind it to the current binding context. The common use case here is partial views:

```
<div class="page-host container">
    <div data-bind="compose: 'shell/sub.html'"></div>
</div>
```

Again, the string could be in the HTML or come from the viewmodel. In this case, as a view is referring to another view, I think the string belongs to the HTML. Otherwise, the reverse violation of the separation of concerns occurs, where a viewmodel has a direct reference to a view.

This sample can be seen in cp5-composition4.

# Explicit models and views

The compose binding can also take a settings object that specifies a model, a view, or both. There isn't much to say about these examples, so this section is taken directly from the Durandal documentation:

- `data-bind="compose: { model: model }"`: This uses the value of `model` with `viewLocator` to obtain a view. They are then bound and the view is injected into the DOM node.

- `data-bind="compose: { view: view }"`: This evaluates the value of `view`. If it is a string, then `viewLocator` is used to locate the view; otherwise, it is assumed to be a view. The resultant view is injected into the DOM node.

- `data-bind="compose: { model: model, view: view }"`: This resolves the value of `model`. The value of `view` is resolved and a view is constructed as indicated in the previous point. Both `model` and `view` are then bound and injected into the DOM node.

- `data-bind="compose: { model: model, view:'myView.html' }"`: The value of `model` is resolved. The `viewLocator` module is then used to obtain the view indicated by the `view` property. They are then bound, and the view is injected into the DOM node.

- `data-bind="compose: { model:'shell', view: view }"`: RequireJS is used to resolve the `shell` module. The value of `view` is resolved and a view is returned, as described in the previous point. The view is then bound to the resolved module and injected into the DOM node.

- `data-bind="compose: { model:'shell', view:'myView.html' }"`: RequireJS is used to resolve the `shell` module. The `viewLocator` module is then used to obtain the view indicated by `view`. The view is then bound to the resolved module and injected into the DOM node.

# Containerless composition

All of the preceding examples work with Knockout's containerless comment syntax as well, so the following is valid:

```
<!-- ko compose: model--><!--/ko-->
```

The composition system has more features than there are in the scope of this chapter, including view caching, transitions, template mode, and custom view location strategies. They will be discussed in the next chapter, which covers more advanced use cases.

# View locations

As mentioned earlier, the default behavior of the `viewLocator` module used by composition is to look for a view with the same path as the module, but with the `.html` extension. This results in modules grouped by folder:

In the preceding example, the `shell` directory contains the view and the viewmodel for the shell, and the `contacts` directory contains a base model for a contact, as well as a view and viewmodel for both `list` and `edit`. I think this organization is very easy to understand, and it scales well with large applications, as each feature or group of features is kept together.

Durandal offers another strategy though, which it calls the conventional strategy. You can activate it by modifying your `main.js` file to call `useConvention` on the `viewlocator` module:

```
define(['durandal/system', 'durandal/app',
    'durandal/viewLocator'],
function(system, app, viewLocator) {

    //plugin configuration omitted

    viewLocator.useConvention('viewmodels', 'views');

    app.title = 'Mastering Knockout';
    app.start().then(function () {
        app.setRoot('shell/shell');
    });
});
```

This causes Durandal to look for a module with the `viewmodels/contactList` ID at `views/contactList.html`. While you can enter any strings for the viewmodels and views, paths, this is actually the default. Calling `viewLocator.useConvention()` (with no parameters) will produce the same effect.

I don't think this method scales as well, and I personally find it harder to work with. I prefer to have the viewmodel and view in the same location in the filesystem, so that I don't have to hunt for it. It's all up to you (or your team's) preference though.

All of the code samples shown here will use the default behavior, not the conventional behavior.

# Using the router

While technically an optional plugin, I don't imagine any real-world SPAs will do without the use of the router. While SammyJS ties a URL fragment to a function, Durandal's router ties the URL directly to a module ID. The module can return either a singleton or a constructor, and will be used to bind the view using the standard composition system.

## Configuring the router

Let's start configuring the router:

1. Route configuration is pretty straightforward. Here is the `shell` module with router configuration for the `Contact` application:

```
define(['plugins/router', 'knockout', 'durandal/app'],
function (router, ko, app) {
  return {
    title: app.title,
    router: router,
    activate: function () {

      router.map([
        { route: '', moduleId: 'contacts/list', title:
          'Contacts', nav: true },
        { route: 'contacts/new', moduleId: 'contacts/edit',
          title: 'New Contact', nav: true },
        { route: 'contacts/:id', moduleId: 'contacts/edit',
          title: 'Contact Details', nav: false }
      ])
      .buildNavigationModel()
      .mapUnknownRoutes('shell/error', 'not-found');
```

```
        return router.activate();
    }
  };
});
```

2. The router plugin is required in the `shell` module and is set up during its `activate` method.

3. The `map` method takes an array of routes and `buildNavigationModel` sets up those routes. The `mapUnknownRoutes` function takes a module ID and a route to use as a catch-all for attempts to navigate to routes that have not been registered. Without this, navigation will be canceled instead, with no error displayed to the user!

4. We will cover `activate` and the other life cycle hooks in detail in a bit. For now, just know that `activate` is called during composition. If the return value from `activate` is a `promise`, then composition will wait until the promise resolves.

5. Finally, `router.activate`, which also returns a `promise`, is returned to the shell's `activate` method, which chains the wait from composition until the router has finished.

# Route properties

The route's configuration objects that are passed to the `map` function take the following properties:

- `route`: This is the URL to map to. It can be a string or an array of strings. Each string can take one of the following forms:
    - Default route: This is `route: ''`.
    - Static route: This is `route: 'contacts'`.
    - Parameterized route: This is `route: 'contacts/:id'`.
    - Optional parameter route: This is `route: 'contacts(/:id)'`.
    - Splat route: This is `route: 'contacts*details'`. It is a *wild card*, and will match any URL starting with `contacts`.

- `moduleId`: This is the module to bind the route to.

- `hash`: This is used primarily for data binding `<a>` tags. In most cases, the router will generate this automatically, but it can be overridden. It is necessary to override this property on routes with optional parameters or splats.

- **title**: The `document.title` property is set to this value. If present, then the route is active; if absent, the `document.title` is not changed.

- **nav**: If `true`, the route will be included in the router's `navigationModel`, an observable array of routes created when `buildNavigationModel` is called, which can be used to easily generate navigation bars. The default value is `false`.

If a module with an `activate` or `canActivate` function is activated by the router, the route's parameters are passed as arguments to it. Again, activation and other life cycle hooks will be covered in more detail later in this chapter.

Query strings are also passed in as the last parameters to `activate`/`canActivate` as objects with a key/value pair query string key.

# Binding the router

The router introduces a special binding, also called **router**, which wraps the compose binding with special handling logic. It shares the same properties as the compose binding:

```
<!-- ko router: { model: router.activeItem }--> <!-- /ko -->
```

The `activeItem` object on the router holds the currently active routes' module. If the `model` property on the router binding is omitted, the binding will look for a router property on the current binding context and take its `activeItem` object. The preceding example is equivalent to this one:

```
<!-- ko router: { }--> <!-- /ko -->
```

The router also has a `navigationModel` observable array, which is very useful in generating navigation bars:

```
<ul class="nav navbar-nav" data-bind="foreach:
  router.navigationModel">
  <li data-bind="css: { active: isActive }">
    <a class="" data-bind="attr: { href: hash }, text: title"></a>
  </li>
</ul>
```

Each route has an `isActive` property, which indicates when the route is active, and a `hash` property, which can be used for a tag's `href` property.

Loading or navigating, are also exposed as observables on the router. This makes it easy to bind loading indicators on the page:

```
<i class="fa fa-spinner fa-3x fa-spin" data-bind="visible:
    router.isNavigating"></i>
```

Okay, time to look at a live example. Open the `cp5-router` branch. Try moving around the application by editing contacts or using the navigation bar links. Notice that the URL's hash is updated to match the current route. You can even use the browsers back and forward buttons to control navigation, as the router is hooked into the `window.location` object. Like all true SPAs, the navigation occurs inside the app, not by performing browser navigation.

# Activating routes

When a route is activated, the associated viewmodel module is loaded with RequireJS and composed into the DOM. The module loaded by RequireJS must either be an object, which will be treated as a singleton and bound to the view, or a function, which will be treated as a constructor and used to `new` up an object to bind to the view.

# Navigation – hash change versus push state

We just saw how the router handled navigation by changing the URL's hash. This is the default behavior, but the router also supports push state navigation. Push state navigation is the use of the HTML5 history API to modify the current URL and the history stack, without causing browser navigation. This results in prettier and normal looking URLs during router navigation. We see `http://localhost:3000/contacts/new` instead of `http://localhost:3000/#contacts/new`.

This mode of navigation can be activated by passing the `router.activate({ pushState: true })` calling. Though older browsers don't support push state, Durandal will gracefully degrade to hash change navigation when push state is not supported.

The reason this isn't the default behavior is because it requires support from the server to work properly. Currently, our server is only serving our application when we navigate to the root URL. If we try to navigate to `/contacts/new`, the server will display a `404` error. As Durandal is supposed to be in control of routes and navigation, adding this support route-by-route to the server would be a lot of duplication. The recommended way to support push state on the server is to use a wild card route to send all page requests to the index page. Once Durandal loads, it will detect the URL and activate the proper route.

The implementation of wild card routes will depend entirely on your server backend. Our examples are using a Node.js server, which makes it pretty easy:

```
//Index Route
app.get('/*', function(req, res){
  res.sendfile(clientDir + '/index.html');
});
```

That will take care of the page routing, but there is a much bigger supportability issue with push state routing; relative paths in HTML and the RequireJS config. Right now, all the links to CSS or the scripts in our code look like this:

```
<link rel="stylesheet" href="content/css/app.css" />
```

This is a problem if the page tries to load /contacts/new, because content/css is a relative path; it will be treated by the browser as /contacts/content/css. Obviously this will fail; either the server will display a 404 error, or worse, the wild card route will cause the index page to be returned!

To fix this, all the paths need to be absolute paths; they have to start with a forward slash (/):

```
<link rel="stylesheet" href="/content/css/app.css" />
```

This one can be nasty as is it requires manually updating any code with links in it, including the RequireJS config. As long as you are aware of the road you want to take when you start a project, this isn't much of a headache. If you can, I recommend going to the push state route. Having those nice looking URLs makes a big difference. It also frees the hash up to do its normal job of indicating a location or state on the page.

You can see an example of the push state scenario in cp5-pushstate. Note that as a special treat, this branch supports IE 8 so that you can see the graceful degradation to hash change navigation. The rest of the examples in this chapter will use push state navigation, but will return only to supporting ES5-compatible browsers.

# Controlling the navigation from JavaScript

Navigation can easily be done with the router's navigate function, which takes a URL string. The router is a singleton, and can be required into any module, using plugins/router:

```
define(['durandal/app', 'knockout', 'services/mock',
  'plugins/router'],
function(app, ko, dataService, router) {
  return function ContactListVM() {
```

```
//…
self.newEntry = function() {
  router.navigate('contacts/new');
};
self.editContact = function(contact) {
  router.navigate('contacts/' + contact.id());
};
};
});
```

# Modal dialogs

After the overuse of modal dialogs in Windows, and alert boxes in early browser applications, modal dialogs have left a bad taste with some developers. However, when used appropriately, they are simple and powerful tools. Durandal's modal dialog implementation makes collecting user input from modals very easy, by making dialogs return promises that resolve when they close. Modal dialogs in Durandal come in two types, namely, message boxes and custom dialogs.

# Message boxes

For simple cases such as displaying a notification or collecting a single piece of user input, Durandal provides a modal dialog on `app.showMessage`, which takes the following parameters:

- `Message (string)`: This contains the main contents of the message box.

- `Title (string, optional)`: This contains the title of the message box; the default title is `app.title`.

- `Buttons (array, optional)`: This is an array of buttons to show; the default is `['Ok']`. The first button in the array will be the default action of the dialog. If the array is an array of strings, then the text will be both the button text and the return value of clicking that button. To specify the value of a button, use an array of objects, that is, `[{ text: "One", value: 1 }, { text: "Two", value: 2 }]`.

- `Autoclose (boolean, optional)`: If `true`, the dialog will be closed if the user clicks outside of the dialog window; the default is `false`.

- `Settings (object, optional)`: See the upcoming *Message box settings* section.

While a simple call to `app.showMessage('This is a message!')` is a good way to put something right in front of the user, I think the best use case for message boxes is the *Are you sure?* confirmation dialog:

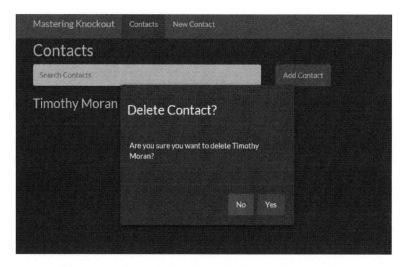

```
self.deleteContact = function(contact) {
  app.showMessage('Are you sure you want to delete ' +
    contact.displayName() + '?', 'Delete Contact?', ['No', 'Yes'])
    .then(function(response) {
      if (response === 'Yes') {
        dataService.removeContact(contact.id(), function() {
          self.contacts.remove(contact);
        });
      }
    });
};
```

Here we are showing a message box when someone tries to delete a contact. The message includes the contact's name (to provide context) and a title. The order of the two buttons, **No** then **Yes**, ensures that if the user hits enter immediately, **No** will be selected. I think it's good to default to the safer case. Whatever the user selects will be given to the promise returned from `showMessage`, which we can access in the `then` handler.

Depending on how you count those lines, we just double-checked a user action with a modal dialog in 2-3 lines of very-readable code. You can see an example of this in the `cp5-message` branch.

# Message box settings

The last parameter to `showMessage` is an object that controls display options. It takes the following parameters:

- `buttonClass`: This specifies a class for all buttons. The default is `btn`.

- `primaryButtonClass`: This specifies an additional class for the first button. The default is `btn-primary`.

- `secondaryButtonClass`: It specifies an additional class for buttons other than the first. The default is no class.

- `class`: This specifies the class of the outermost `div` element of the message box. The default is `"messageBox"`. Note that you must specify this property with quotes or it will crash in IE8; for example, `"class"` and `"myClass"`.

- `style`: This specifies additional styles for the outermost `div` element of the message box. The default is nothing.

You can also control the default settings by passing the same settings object to `dialog.MessageBox.setDefaults`. This function will merge the settings passed to it with the defaults; if you leave settings out, they will be left alone, not removed.

# Custom dialogs

Message boxes are great for single input such as yes, no, or choosing an option from a list. However, when things need to get more complex than a single answer, Durandal allows us to create custom dialogs. To show a custom dialog, you can require the dialog object with `plugins/dialog` and call `dialog.show`, or use the alias `app.showDialog`. Dialogs use composition, so any viewmodel passed to `show` will look up and bind against its view using the standard methods.

To close itself and pass a result back to the caller, the dialog-hosted viewmodel will need to require `plugins/dialog` and call `dialog.close(self, result)`.

To see how this works, open the `cp5-dialog` branch. The **Add Contact** button on the main list page will open the edit viewmodel in a dialog, which will either close with `null` for a canceled entry or a new contact for the saved entry. Just to show how flexible it is, the Add Contact link in the nav bar will still navigate to a new page to create a new contact. Both, the dialog and the page are run by the same viewmodel!

```
define(['durandal/system', 'knockout', 'plugins/router',
  'services/mock', 'contacts/contact', 'plugins/dialog'],
function(system, ko, router, dataService, Contact, dialog) {
  return function EditContactVm(init) {
    var self = this;
```

```
    self.contact = ko.observable(new Contact());

    self.activate = function(id) {
      //Id is only present when editing
      if (id)
        dataService.getContact(id, self.contact);
    };

    self.saveEntry = function() {
      var action = self.contact().id() === 0
        ? dataService.createContact
        : dataService.updateContact;

      action(self.contact(), function() {
        self.close(self.contact());
      });
    };

    self.cancel = function() {
      self.close(null);
    };

    self.close = function(result) {
      if (dialog.getDialog(self))
        dialog.close(self, result);
      else
        router.navigate('');
    };
  };
});
```

As you can see, almost nothing has changed. Instead of always using the router to navigate home when finished, the new close method checks `dialog.getDialog(self))` to see whether it is a dialog, and closes itself with the result (null or the newly created contact). The `dialog.getDialog(self))` method returns the dialog context, or is undefined if none is found.

The list viewmodel has to only make the following change to open the dialog and keep the result:

```
self.newEntry = function() {
  app.showDialog(new ContactVM())
  .then(function(newContact) {
    if (newContact) {
```

```
        self.contacts.push(newContact);
      }
    });
  };
```

The `ContactVM` object is the edit viewmodel, which is being required in with `contact/edit`. A new one is constructed and passed to `app.showDialog`. Composition renders the viewmodel and returns the promise for the dialog's result. This promise will be completed by the `dialog.close` call in the edit viewmodel. The `then` handler just checks to make sure it exists and adds it to its list of contacts.

There are some HTML/CSS considerations with custom dialogs. Unlike message boxes, which are styled with Bootstrap's modal classes by Durandal, custom dialogs are rendered into an empty `div` element that is centered with absolute positioning and a transparent background. Without some styling, the output looks pretty terrible:

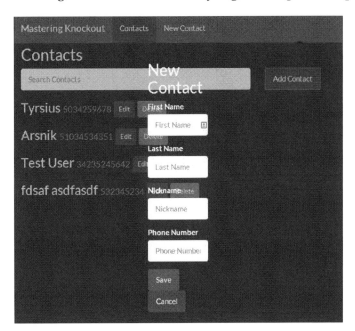

Thankfully, it doesn't take much to clean this up. This is the CSS I used:

```
.edit-container {
  padding: 20px;
  min-width: 600px;
  background-color: #222222;
}
```

The preceding CSS produces this much nicer looking result:

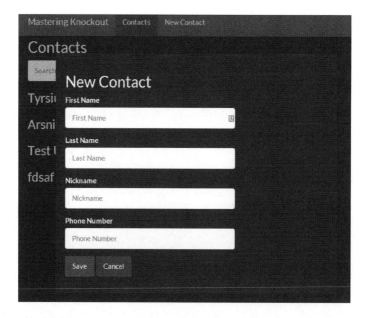

While the need for this might be surprising, I think it's better than the alternative where Durandal does apply some default styling to all modals, which has to forcefully be overridden when it doesn't match what you want. In the next chapter, we will cover adding custom dialog hosts, which provides a much nicer way to control default modal appearance for both message boxes and custom dialogs.

## An alternative method

To keep the calling viewmodel a little cleaner and less aware of how the dialog viewmodel works, I prefer to encapsulate the actual dialog code. This is easy to do by adding a `show` method to the edit viewmodel:

```
self.show = function() {
  return dialog.show(self);
};
```

And calling it instead of `app.showDialog`, as seen here:

```
self.newEntry = function() {
  new ContactVM().show()
  .then(function(newContact) {
    if (newContact) {
```

```
        self.contacts.push(newContact);
      }
    });
  };
```

This hides the specific method from the caller, allowing the edit viewmodel to control how it shows itself. The `show` method could even take the parameters that allowed configuration before showing the dialog. This is especially useful when multiple dialog hosts are available, which we will cover in the next chapter. You can see this example in the `cp5-dailog2` branch.

# The application's life cycle

Durandal's composition and activator services allow optional callbacks to control or hook into their life cycles. They can be useful when performing setup and teardown, or implementing logic to block or redirect page changes.

# The activation life cycle

An activator is a special computed observable, whose `write` function enforces the activation life cycle. Unless you are managing composition or routing yourself, the only activators you will work with are the ones used by the router and the dialog system. Though, if you are interested, you can create your own activator by requiring in the `durandal/activator` module and using the `create` function.

The following optional properties are called by the activator when the active value tries to change:

- `canActivate`: This is called on the new value; it should return either a Boolean or a promise that resolves to a Boolean. If the result is `false`, activation is cancelled.

- `activate`: This is called on the new value after `canActivate`; it is used to perform any desired setup logic. If activate returns a promise, the new value will not become the active value until the promise resolves.

- `canDeactivate`: This is called on the old value; just like activate, it should return either a Boolean or a promise that resolves to a Boolean. If the result is false, activation is cancelled.

- `Deactivate`: This is called on the old value after activation succeeds, but before the switch is made. It is used to perform any teardown logic.

# Preparing viewmodels with activate

You have already seen the use of `activate` in the list and edit viewmodels, where it is used to load data:

```
self.activate = function() {
  dataService.getContacts(function(contacts) {
    self.contacts(contacts);
  });
};
```

What probably hasn't been obvious, because the mock data service is using local storage, is that if this service call actually took time, the page would render before the data got back. This could result in a jarring change when all of the contacts suddenly load. The `activate` call isn't waiting for this callback to finish, so Durandal is activating the viewmodel before it's really ready.

To see what this looks like, open the `cp5-timeout` branch. All the mock service calls have had a 1 second timeout added before their callbacks are used, which will result in a more real-world response time scenario. Loading the home page, you can see the list load after the rest of the page. This is especially problematic when trying to edit a contact, as the form will show the default values until the contact is loaded.

To stop the page loading until the list is retrieved, we can return a promise from activate. The `durandal/system` module provides a way to create promises if you aren't using your own library (such as Q) to do so:

```
self.activate = function() {
  return system.defer(function(defer) {
    dataService.getContacts(function(contacts) {
      self.contacts(contacts);
      defer.resolve();
    });
  }).promise();
};
```

Here, we are returning a promise that will be resolved by the callback to our mock data service. The `system.defer` function takes a handler that performs asynchronous working, calling it with a deferred object. The deferred object has the resolve and reject functions, which can take values for success or failure. You can see this in the `cp5-activate` branch, where the same change was made for the edit page. As activate is waiting on this promise, activation will not continue until it resolves. These pages will not activate until their data is loaded, so the user never sees the page before it is ready.

While this method works, there is a cleaner way to do it. Instead of using callbacks in our data service and promises in our viewmodels, which really mixes strategies, we can use promises in our data service. If our data service returns a promise, the activate method looks much nicer:

```
self.activate = function() {
  return dataService.getContacts()
  .then(function(contacts) {
    self.contacts(contacts);
  });
};
```

What an improvement! In fact, we can take it even further. As `self.contacts` is an observable array, which is just a function, we can cut out the anonymous function in the `then` handler with this shorthand:

```
self.activate = function() {
  return dataService.getContacts()
  .then(self.contacts);
};
```

This works because `self.contacts` becomes the `then` handler, so when the service returns the list of contacts, the promise resolves directly into it. This doesn't appeal to everyone, and it might even look confusing. However, if it doesn't impair readability for you, the shorter code might be nice.

This method can be seen in the `cp5-activate2` branch, which fully converts all the data access code into promises, such as this one:

```
getContacts: function() {
  return system.defer(function(defer) {
    //Return our POJO contacts as real contact objects
    var typedContacts = [];
    for (var c in contacts) {
      if (contacts.hasOwnProperty(c)) {
        typedContacts.push(new Contact(contacts[c]))
      }
    }
    setTimeout(function() {
      defer.resolve(typedContacts);
    }, 1000);
  }).promise();
}
```

Because Durandal has this understanding of promises integrated into its life cycle hooks, it makes using promises for all asynchronous code that much more appealing. If you aren't doing this already, I strongly encourage you to consider it. All code samples from here on will be using promises.

This asynchronous activation is another advantage of the composition of components. Components can only construct and bind synchronously, which can make some components very tricky to initialize. Composition allows asynchronous work to be done, making it that much more flexible.

# A note on the router's isNavigating property

In the previous section, *Binding the router*, we looked at the `isNavigating` property of the router, which is `true` during navigation. The activation life cycle is part of navigation, so `isNavigating` will be `true` during any asynchronous activity in the activation life cycle. This allows you to bind visual indicators on the page while your pages are loading, making your application feel more responsive.

# Checking navigation with canDeactivate

The `canActivate` and `canDeactivate` methods also support promises. Going off to the server with an Ajax request to see whether a view can be deactivated might seem weird, but Ajax isn't the only source of promises. Perhaps the best possible use case for `canDeactivate` is with the promise from a simple message box—**You have unsaved changes, are you sure you want to leave?**

Open the `cp5-deactivate` branch and open up a contact to edit. If you hit **Cancel**, you will still be taken back to the list, but if you make changes and hit **Cancel**, you will be prompted. If you hit **No**, navigation will be cancelled.

You might think that this is being done from the **Cancel** button, but it will also happen if the user clicks on the browser's back button or the navigation link (basically, anything but a hard browser navigation). This is because `canDeactivate` is run no matter what source the attempted deactivation comes from:

```
self.canDeactivate = function() {
  if (!self.contact().state.isDirty())
  return true;
  return app.showMessage('You have unsaved changes. Are you sure
    you want to leave?', 'Cancel Edit?', ['No', 'Yes'])
  .then(function(response) {
    return response === 'Yes';
  });
};
```

The dirty flag in this sample is taken from Ryan Niemeyer's blog *Knock Me Out* at `http://www.knockmeout.net/2011/05/creating-smart-dirty-flag-in-knockoutjs.html`. It can be seen in the `common/extensions.js` file in the branch source code.

Here, we are just showing a standard message box and transforming the result into a Boolean for `canDeactivate`. The promise for this result is returned, and `canDeactivate` will wait until it resolves, to determine whether or not activation can continue.

We can actually shorten this, because the activator module will interpret the strings' responses by checking them against a list of affirmations and responses that it considers to be true. This is the code Durandal uses to check activation results, taken from the activator module:

```
affirmations: ['yes', 'ok', 'true'],
interpretResponse: function(value) {
  if(system.isObject(value)) {
    value = value.can || false;
  }

  if(system.isString(value)) {
     return ko.utils.arrayIndexOf(this.affirmations, value.
toLowerCase()) !== -1;
  }

  return value;
}
```

This array of `truthy` strings can be changed by accessing `activator.defaults.affirmations`.

With this knowledge, we can just return the promise from the message box directly. The activator module will consider `Yes` to be a truthy result, and any other string to be `false`:

```
self.canDeactivate = function() {
  if (!self.contact().state.isDirty())
    return true;
  return app.showMessage('You have unsaved changes. Are you sure
    you want to leave?', 'Cancel Edit?', ['No', 'Yes']);
};
```

Doesn't that look nice? You can see this in the `cp5-deactivate2` branch.

While these examples are short, hopefully, they give you an idea of what the activation life cycle is capable of, especially when combined with promises. Because promises can be chained, you could block deactivation when you go to the server to get some information, then display it to the user in a message box, and pass the result to the activator module.

# Composition

The composition life cycle has another set of events that can be hooked into, which allow you to control how the DOM is rendered, or respond to various stages of composition. Again, all of these are optional:

- `getView()`: This is a function that can return a view ID (path to a view file), or a DOM element. This overrides any other view location done by composition.

- `viewUrl`: This is a string property of a view ID, to override view location. It will only be used if `getView` is not present.

- `activate()`: Just like activation's `activate` method, this function will be called when composition begins. If the compose binding has an `activationData` method specified, it will be given to activate as a parameter. If a promise is returned, the composition will not continue until it resolves.

- `binding(view)`: This is called before binding occurs. The view is passed to this function as a parameter. If binding returns `false` or `{ applyBindings:false }`, binding will not be done on the view.

- `bindingComplete(view)`: This is called when binding finishes. The view is passed as a parameter.

- `attached(view, parent)`: This is called with the view and its parent DOM element after it is added to the DOM.

- `compositionComplete(view, parent)`: This is called with the view and its parent DOM element after all composition, including the composition of child elements, has been completed.

- `detached(view, parent)`: This is called after the view has been removed from the DOM.

In the case of the combined activation and composition life cycles, such as the router's navigation, the activation module's `activate` method is the only one called.

With the exception of binding, which can stop binding from occurring, the composition life cycle hooks do not offer the opportunity to control or cancel the process like the activation hooks do. Though it is generally discouraged in MVVM for the viewmodel to interact directly with the view, the composition life cycle is designed to make it easy to do so. Patterns should only be followed as long as they are helpful or possible, and if binding just can't get your work done, you may need to work with the DOM in your viewmodel.

# Widgets

Widgets in Durandal are similar to Knockout components, in that they are viewmodel/view pairs that are instantiated from the DOM. Components use a custom element while widgets use a custom binding. There is definitely some overlap between them, but Durandal's widget system came before Knockout's component system. Widgets also have a killer feature over components; their views can have replaceable sections that can be overridden. This feature is commonly known as **transclusion**—the inclusion of one document inside another.

It's difficult to talk about the widget API without using an example. When we looked at components, we made a contact list component; so let's see what it would look like doing the same thing with a widget. It may not be very reusable, making it an odd choice for a widget; but it will cover the whole process.

## Creating a new widget

Durandal expects widgets to be located in a directory named `widgets`, at the root of your app, which, in our case, would be under `client/app/widgets`. Each widget will store its code in a folder, which will be used as the name of the widget. The code for a widget must be a JavaScript file named `viewmodel.js` and an HTML file named `view.html`. So to make our contacts list item widget, we will use the following structure:

For the view, we are just going to pull the whole list section out of the
`list.html` view:

```
<ul class="list-unstyled" data-bind="foreach: contacts">
  <li>
    <h3>
    <span data-bind="text: displayName"></span> <small data-
      bind="text: phoneNumber"></small>
    <button class="btn btn-sm btn-default" data-bind="click:
      $parent.edit">Edit</button>
    <button class="btn btn-sm btn-danger" data-bind="click:
      $parent.delete">Delete</button>
    </h3>
  </li>
</ul>
```

As we are going to be binding against a new viewmodel, I've changed the `foreach`
binding from `displayContacts` to `contacts`. Our viewmodel is going to look very
similar to our normal page viewmodels. Like pages instantiated by the router, our
widget's viewmodel won't be able to receive construction parameters; data passed
to the widget through the binding will be given to the `activate` function:

```
define(['durandal/app', 'knockout'], function(app, ko) {
  return function ContactListWidget() {
    var self = this;

    self.activate = function(options) {
      self.contacts = options.data;
      self.edit = options.edit;
      self.delete = options.delete;
    };
  };
});
```

We are passing in the data the view needs here, that is, the `contacts` array, and a
callback for `edit` and `delete`.

# Using a widget

Durandal provides several ways to use the widget. First, we have to activate the
widget plugin in our `main.js` file:

```
app.configurePlugins({
  //Durandal plugins
  router:true,
```

```
    dialog: true,
    widget: true
});
```

Now we can use the widget binding to create the widget:

```
<div data-bind="widget: { kind: 'contactList',
   data: displayContacts,
  edit: editContact,
  delete: deleteContact }">
</div>
```

I don't really like this though; it's a little verbose. There are two ways to register the widget, which allow it to be used as if it was a binding itself:

```
<div data-bind="contactList: { data: displayContacts,
  edit: editContact,
  delete: deleteContact }">
</div>
```

I think this looks much nicer. To register a widget, you can either call `widget.registerKind('contactList')`, or modify the plugin configuration:

```
app.configurePlugins({
  //Durandal plugins
  router:true,
  dialog: true,
  widget: {
    kinds: ['contactList']
  }
});
```

I personally prefer this last method; though if you have a lot of widgets, you might prefer one of the other methods. You can see this widget being used in the `cp5-widget` branch. The result looks identical to the previous version, but the list is now in a separate view.

# Modifying widgets with data-part attributes

So far, there isn't much to our widget. It doesn't add anything that a Knockout component couldn't have given us, and the components have the nicer looking custom element syntax going for them.

If you have an element in your widget's view with a `data-part` attribute, then that element can be overridden by the caller. Let's say, for example, that we wanted to be able to change the way the phone number was displayed. The first step is to add a `data-part` attribute to the widget:

```
<small data-bind="text: phoneNumber" data-part="phone"></small>
```

The next step is to use the same `data-part` attribute in the caller:

```
<div data-bind="contactList: { data: displayContacts,
   edit: editContact,
   delete: deleteContact }">
   <span data-part="phone" data-bind="text: phoneNumber"></span>
</div>
```

The result is the new `span` element that replaces the original small element inside the widget. You can see this in the `cp5-datapart` branch.

An important thing to notice here is that the new `span` element has a data binding that refers to a contact's `phoneNumber` property. The `data-part` attribute is overriding an element whose binding context is in the scope of the `foreach` loop of the widget, and this scope is maintained by the new element. The binding context of a `data-part` attribute, declared inside of a widget-bound element, is the binding context of the element it replaces.

The special `$root` property of a widget's binding context is set to the declaring scope, which is especially handy for overriding `data-part` attributes. If we want to refer to properties on the list viewmodel, we can do so:

```
<div data-bind="contactList: { data: displayContacts, delete:
   deleteContact }">

   <small data-part="phone"><em data-bind="text:
   phoneNumber"></em></small>
   <button data-part="edit-btn" data-bind="click: $root.editContact
   " class="btn btn-sm btn-default">Edit</button>
</div>
```

This assumes that the matching button in the widget view has the `data-part=
"edit-btn"` attribute added to it. This button now directly references the `editContact` function on the list viewmodel, instead of the one on the widget. You can see this in action in the `cp5-datapart2` branch.

A widget can have any number of `data-part` attributes, and each `data-part` attribute can contain other `data-part` attributes. This allows maximum flexibility in controlling the appearance and functionality of templated widgets.

# Summary

These are just the basics of using Durandal, but hopefully you can already appreciate the power and simplicity the framework provides. It frequently happens online that Knockout is compared to more complete frameworks such as Angular, and where it lacks components, such as a router, they are taken as points against it. Durandal stacks up much more evenly with these frameworks while it still takes advantage of all of the things that make Knockout great.

In this chapter, you should have learned the composition system, as well as how the router brings organization and modularity to your application. We saw how promises combine with modal dialogs and the application life cycle to allow us to respond to asynchronous events easily and naturally. Finally, we saw how widgets can take the concepts behind Knockout components (reusable behavior-driven controls that are instantiated from the view markup) and add templated `data-part` attributes to achieve transclusion.

The next chapter will continue to explore how the Durandal framework simplifies Knockout application development.

# 6
# Advanced Durandal

In the previous chapter, we covered most of the basic uses of the Durandal framework. By now, you should feel comfortable starting an application with it. In this chapter, we will continue to look at Durandal by covering some more advanced framework features as well as looking at some useful patterns that will help us solve common challenges encountered in the SPA development.

- Publishing and subscribing with events
- Application login scenarios
- Advanced composition
- Nested routers
- Custom modal dialogs
- Binding to plain JavaScript objects

## Publishing and subscribing

A very common problem new developers face when they start using Knockout is how to communicate between viewmodels without establishing a single hierarchy with a master viewmodel or any other form of direct reference between viewmodel objects. These kind of hard dependencies are generally considered bad practice, but the need to send messages between different viewmodels is unavoidable.

The publish-subscribe (pub/sub) pattern is a popular solution to this problem. Durandal offers you a simple pub/sub implementation via the `Events` module. There are two ways in which you can use the events system: with the events included on the `durandal/app` object by default or by adding events to your own objects.

# The events module

The events system includes the `events` module and the `subscription` class. The `events` module, required by `durandal/events`, provides you with the `includeIn` method to add events to an object. When `Events.includeIn(obj)` is called, the following functions are added to `obj`:

- `on`: This is used to subscribe to events on the object
- `off`: This is used to unsubscribe to events
- `trigger`: This is used to raise events
- `proxy`: This returns a function that can be called to raise events

## Subscribing to events

The `on` method can be used in two different ways. To provide a callback and an optional context (a `this` value for the callback), pass them in as parameters. From `on`, `obj` will be returned so that chained subscriptions can be added:

```
obj.on('contact:added', self.contacts.push, self.contacts)
.on('contact:deleted', self.contacts.remove, self.contacts);
```

To get a subscription object, provide only the event name to `on`. What is returned from `on` will be a subscription object, which provides a `then` and an `off` method. The `then` method can be used to attach a callback:

```
obj.on('contact:added').then(function(newContact) {
  self.contacts.push(newContact);
});
```

The `then` method also returns the subscription that allows you to store the subscription reference.

You can subscribe to multiple events simultaneously using a space-delimited list of names for the event name parameter. You can also subscribe to all events on the object using the `all` event name.

## Unsubscribing from events

Removing a callback is done in a manner that is similar to adding callbacks, and it depends on whether you added the callback with `on` or by using `then` on a subscription.

If you subscribed with on, you can unsubscribe by calling off with the same event name and callback. To remove all callbacks for that event name (or names), do not provide a callback to the second parameter. To remove all callbacks with a specific context, provide a context to the third parameter:

```
//Remove a specific callback on an event
obj.off('contact:added', self.contacts.push);

//Remove all callbacks for a context (will remove both added and
  deleted from above example)
obj.off(undefined, undefined, self.contacts);

//Remove all callbacks
obj.off();
```

If you used a subscription object, just call off on the subscription:

```
var subscription = obj.on('contact:added')
  .then(self.contacts.push);
//unsubscribe
sSubscription.off();
```

# Raising events

Triggering events on an object is similar to subscribing to them. You can use a single event name, multiple space-delimited event names, or trigger all events using the special all event name.

When events are triggered, they can pass along parameters to the callbacks of subscribing events. Though triggered events can use any number of parameters, it is much easier to work with callbacks when they always use a single parameter:

```
obj.trigger('contact:added', newContact);
obj.trigger('contact:added contact:approved', newApprovedContact);
obj.trigger('all', superImportantEventData);
```

# Proxying events

An event proxy is a method that will raise a preselected event (or a list of events), passing along its arguments as the event parameters. The following two methods are equivalent:

```
obj.trigger('contact:added', newContact);
//
var contactAdded = obj.proxy('contact:added');
contactAdded(newContact);
```

The benefit of proxies is that they are reusable, and they can be stored or passed around. This is useful in order to share the proxy with other systems or just have a single event-raising function in several places. This practice of creating a function to represent another function with a fixed parameter is known as **currying**.

The event name of a proxy can be any string that `trigger` can use, including `all`.

# Application events

As the `app` object is a singleton that has events included out of the box, its events are useful for application-wide messaging. Communication between independent top-level components, such as page viewmodels, is a good candidate for app-wide messaging.

Let's say we wanted to reduce load on the server by raising an event when a new contact was added so that the list page could get the new contact without going to the server to refresh the whole list. To stop loading the list during it's `activate` method, it will be converted into a singleton that reuses the same loading promise:

```
function ContactListVM() {
  // ...
  var singleActivate = dataService.getContacts()
  .then(function(contacts) {
    self.contacts(contacts);
  });

  self.activate = function() {
    return singleActivate;
  };
  //...
};

return new ContactListVM();
```

As the promise that is returned to `activate` is only run once, the list will not be reloaded when the page is navigated multiple times.

The list page's viewmodel now needs to create an event subscription in order to receive new contacts. Durandal's convention for event names is to specify the source(s) and event type, separated by colons. This convention is recommended but not required; Durandal does not treat colons as delimiters for event names. For example, these are two events raised by the router during the navigation:

```
router:navigation:complete
router:navigation:cancelled
```

To subscribe to an event for a new contact, the list page can use the following subscription:

```
app.on('contact:added').then(function(newContact) {
  self.contacts.push(newContact);
});
```

However, because the only action being taken is to send the `newContact` parameter to `contacts.push`, it would be shorter to write it as a callback with a context:

```
app.on('contact:added', self.contacts.push, self.contacts);
```

These two methods are equivalent. It should be noted that the third parameter that defines the context is necessary; otherwise, the `push` function will be called and will fail without being in the context of the contacts array.

The new/edit page can now publish this event using the `contact:added` event after it creates a contact:

```
self.saveEntry = function() {
  if (self.contact().id() === 0) {
    dataService.createContact(self.contact())
    .then(function(contact) {
      app.trigger('contact:added', contact);
    });
  } else {
    //Edit
  }
};
```

This will send you the contact returned from the `createContact` promise as the data for the triggered event. However, as this is another case of sending a parameter to another single function, it can be written using a proxy:

```
var contactAdded = app.proxy('contact:added');
self.saveEntry = function() {
  if (self.contact().id() === 0) {
  dataService.createContact(self.contact())
    .then(contactAdded)
  } else {
    //edit
  }
};
```

You can see an example of this in the `cp6-pubsub` branch.

# Module-scoped events

In addition to application-wide pub/sub, Durandal provides a simple method to add the events methods to any object, allowing events to be scoped. Calling `Events.includeIn(obj)` will create the same event handling methods that the `app` object has by default: `on`, `off`, `trigger`, and `proxy`.

The data service is a good candidate for events related to contacts being added (or modified), as only the modules that already have a reference to it will be interested in these events. Moving the `contact:added` event out of the new/edit page into the data service also ensures that the event will still go off if another module tries to add a contact:

```
var dataService = {};
Events.includeIn(dataService);
//other methods omitted
dataService.createContact = function(contact) {
  contact.id(UUID.generate());
  contacts[contact.id()] = ko.toJS(contact);
  saveAllContacts();
  return getTimeoutPromise(contact).then(function() {
    dataService.trigger('contact:added', contact);
    return contact;
  });
};
```

This will add the event methods to the `dataService` object and raise the `contact:added` event in the return promise for the `createContact` method.

The change to the list page viewmodel is just referencing the `dataService` object instead of `app` for the event subscription:

```
dataService.on('contact:added', self.contacts.push,
  self.contacts);
```

That's all that needs to be done. The `dataService` object is now acting as an event scope for contacts. You can see this example in the `cp6-event` branch.

# Handling logins

Handling logins can be tricky for a variety of reasons, and there are hundreds of different techniques out there. Web application login generally falls in one of two categories: either your site is free to browse without being logged in (anytime login), or it uses and requires the user to log in first (gated login). The challenges presented by each category are different, and so are the best solutions.

# Gated login

Until fairly recently, almost all gated login sites used some redirection pattern to present a login page to users, which was usually an unpleasant experience. Beyond the issue of page load time, getting back to the originally requested URL generally meant query string parameters that contained the original URL. If the original URL had query strings itself, they were either lost or appended to the URL query value.

SPAs can sidestep the redirection problem by just showing a login page at the current URL; no redirection means the whole process is faster, there is no hassle with the query string, and the user isn't jarred by the URL changing. They have a different challenge, though: what do you do with the shell? You can place the login form alongside the shell and switch between them with bindings, but this clutters the shell with login markup. You can use a modal dialog to show the login form so that the shell is untouched, but then the shell is either blank or shows information that should be login-gated.

Durandal's `setRoot` method really simplifies this problem. If the user needs to log in, setting the login form as the root means the shell is never even loaded. After the login finishes, the shell can then be set as the root; the shell's markup is left untouched, and the user never sees anything they shouldn't:

1. First, our application startup in `main.js` will use `setRoot` to go to either the login or the shell, depending on whether the user is already logged in (say, from a cookie):

```
define(['durandal/system', 'durandal/app',
   'common/extensions', 'services/mock'],
function(system, app, extensions, dataService) {

  ///Same as before

  app.title = 'Mastering Knockout';
  app.start().then(function () {
    app.setRoot(dataService.isLoggedIn() ? 'shell/shell' :
      'login/page');
  });
});
```

2. This relies on the `dataService` object, performing a synchronous check to see if `isLoggedIn` is `true`, but it can easily support an asynchronous one that's just hooking into the `app.start` promise:

```
app.start()
.then(dataService.isLoggedIn)
.then(function (isLoggedIn) {
  app.setRoot(isLoggedIn ? 'shell/shell' : 'login/page');
});
```

Once the login process is complete, the login viewmodel can just call `setRoot` for the shell. That's it! In fact, the only other properties in the login viewmodel are the ones for `username`, `password`, and a failed sign-in flag. After the login completes, the shell will start up just like it did previously, activate the router, and compose the correct page. There is no need to worry about managing an empty state while the login happens, as the shell is never loaded until `setRoot` is called on it.

You can see an example of this in the `cp6-login` branch. The login module contains a standard viewmodel and view. To log in, use any login details where the username and password are the same. Obviously, in a real application, you would want to create a server request.

One thing that is important to note is the logout function. It's in the shell in the sample, but in a real application, it should be refactored into an external service — probably the same one that holds the methods used to get and set the login cookie in order to centralize the login behaviors. In SPAs, because navigation isn't occurring, it can be a challenge to clean up all of the data a logged-in user has in the application state, especially when you have singletons. Trying to create a cleanup method that removes all of this data is prone to errors; it's easy to miss out on important bits of data, and it requires constant maintenance as the application grows. Instead, it's much safer to just reload the browser. Navigation, even if it's a refresh, completely resets the JavaScript state, guaranteeing that nothing from the previously logged-in user is left in the memory. The `location.reload` method is a simple way to do this, but it might not be the best approach if the user is on a page with a sensitive URL. A safer approach would be to set the location to the domain root:

```
location.href = '/';
```

# Anytime login

Sites that allow users to browse and optionally log in have different challenges compared to gated login sites. Some sites that allow optional login still have a separate login page and still use redirection parameters to get the user back to their original location, but this experience is even more unpleasant for the user, as it seems unnecessary. Of course, it might be required if you allow browsing over HTTP and require a redirect for HTTPS to perform the login, but this is all the more reason to always require HTTPS! If you take the redirection route to get to an HTTPS page, then even the preceding method will not work for you, as the preceding method doesn't use browser navigation to change the page.

If you always require HTTPS for normal browsing, then you can allow the user to log in without interfering with the current page. You can use the same technique that gated login uses, but without the need to hide post-login information, there are less intrusive methods.

A common method, and one of the least intrusive, is to include an inline login form in the navigation bar.

Once logged in, the navigation bar would appear the same as the previous navigation bar with the login name and the logout button. This small section of the navigation bar can be backed by a login viewmodel that is composed into the shell, which keeps the login implementation details separate:

```
<nav role="navigation" class="collapse navbar-collapse"
  id="navbar-collapse-group">
  <ul class="nav navbar-nav" data-bind="foreach:
    router.navigationModel">
    <li data-bind="css: { active: isActive }">
      <a class="" data-bind="attr: { href: hash }, text:
        title"></a>
    </li>
  </ul>
  <div class="nav navbar-nav navbar-right">
    <!-- ko compose: login --><!-- /ko -->
  </div>
</nav>
```

The login viewmodel doesn't need to change much for this, but the logout functionality can be moved into it as it no longer is controlled by the shell. You can see an example of this in the `cp6-login-nav` branch. Try logging in and notice how the navigation bar changes.

## Responding to the user's login changes

The inline login form works, but it is likely that your application will need to respond to the newly logged-in user in some way, for example, letting only logged in users create, edit, or delete contacts. There are two ways to handle this: either use some combination of events and Knockout observables to update the page, or reload the page when the user logs in.

It might be simpler to take the page reload route, but it really depends on your application. If you use anytime login and allow users to see most pages without being logged in, you might not be maintaining two separate versions of each page. Instead, you might have if/visible bindings hiding the logged-in-only content. If that is the case, then updating these observables won't be too much effort.

However, if you are maintaining two separate versions of each page because they are different enough for logged-in users, the page reload method is a better bet. As the reload route doesn't take much explaining, let's look at the first case.

For the simple case of hiding the edit controls, Knockout observables are perfectly sufficient. The login-checking function in the data service is a good place to put observables that multiple viewmodels will depend on, as it is already a shared component. In a larger application, you might want to separate the data service into multiple services in order to serve specific roles such as login and contact CRUD:

```
dataService.loginName = ko.observable(storage.get('loginToken'));
dataService.isLoggedIn = ko.computed(function() {
  return dataService.loginName() != null;
});
dataService.tryLogin = function(username, password) {
  var success = username === password;
  if (success) {
    storage.set('loginToken', username);
    dataService.loginName(username);
  }

  return getTimeoutPromise(success);
};
dataService.logout = function() {
  dataService.loginName(null);
  storage.remove('loginToken');
};
```

Here, loginName determines whether or not isLoggedIn is true. The loginName parameter is set initially if storage has a saved token, and it is updated when the user logs in or out. There are three places that need to use one of these fields: the list page, the list items, and the shell. The list page will use it to expose whether or not a user can edit contacts:

```
self.canEdit = ko.computed(function() {
  return dataService.isLoggedIn();
});
```

This property is used by the list of items in order to hide or show the buttons:

```
<!-- ko if: $parent.canEdit -->
  <button class="btn btn-sm btn-default" data-part="edit-btn"
    data-bind="click: $parent.editContact">Edit</button>
  <button class="btn btn-sm btn-danger" data-bind="click:
    $parent.deleteContact">Delete</button>
<!-- /ko -->
```

For additional safety, the methods backing these buttons should also check the `canEdit` property. The `delete` button is not shown, but it uses the same check as what is shown in the following code:

```
self.editContact = function(contact) {
  if (!self.canEdit()) {
    return;
  }
  router.navigate('contacts/' + contact.id());
};
```

Likewise, to ensure that the user cannot get to the edit page by manually entering the URL, it should use a `canActivate` check to block navigation for anonymous users:

```
self.canActivate = function() {
  return dataService.isLoggedIn();
};
```

Finally, the shell will want to remove the route from the navigation bar when the user is not logged in. One way to do this is to create a computed observable array on the shell that filters out routes when the user isn't logged in:

```
router.map([
  { route: '', moduleId: 'contacts/list', title: 'Contacts', nav:
    true },
  { route: 'contacts/new', moduleId: 'contacts/edit', title: 'New
    Contact', nav: true, auth: true },
  { route: 'contacts/:id', moduleId: 'contacts/edit', title:
    'Contact Details', nav: false }
])
.buildNavigationModel()
.mapUnknownRoutes('shell/error', 'not-found');

this.navigationModel = ko.computed(function() {
  var navigationModel = router.navigationModel();
  if (dataService.isLoggedIn()) {
    return navigationModel;
  } else
```

```
    return navigationModel.filter(function(route) {
      return !route.auth;
    });
  });
```

This model will remove any route with an `auth: true` property when the user is not logged in, which makes it easy to add pages that require login in the future.

This example can be seen in the `cp6-login-event` branch. To make it easy to see the logout transition, this branch does not reload the page when the user logs out; instead, it just clears storage and updates the observables on the data service.

# Guarded routes

In the previous section, we used a `canActivate` check on a page viewmodel to ensure that users could only get to the page when they were logged in. This works, but if multiple pages need to be gated, or we need to use logic that the page might not have, it is possible to add this logic to the router.

The `guardRoute` method is an optional method that the router will use to screen every attempted navigation. It receives the module being activated and the route instruction as parameters. If `true`, or a promise for true, is returned from `guardRoute`, then navigation continues normally. If a string or a promise for a string is returned, it will be used as a redirection route. If `false` or a promise for false is returned, then navigation is cancelled:

```
  router.guardRoute = function(model, instruction) {
    return !(instruction.config.auth && !dataService.isLoggedIn());
  };
```

This router guard can replace the `canActivate` method on the edit page, as it will cancel navigation when the route has `auth:true` and the user is not logged in. However, canceling navigation can sometimes appear to users as the application not responding, such as when the back button is pressed. It can be improved by redirecting the current page to the error page instead:

```
  router.guardRoute = function(model, instruction) {
    return !(instruction.config.auth && !dataService.isLoggedIn())
      || 'shell/error';
  };
```

This example can be seen in the `cp6-guard-route` branch.

# Advanced composition

In *Chapter 5, Durandal – the Knockout Framework*, we covered the basic and common uses of Durandal's composition system. This section will cover further composition techniques such as caching, transitions, and composition mode.

# View caching

By default, the view rendered by the composition binding is discarded when the composed module is changed. This results in the DOM contents of the composition binding always being only the current module's view. The `cacheView` option on the composed binding will change this behavior so that Durandal can keep any view composed. If a module is reactivated using the same object that is already bound to a view, it will not be recreated. Both the `compose` and `router` bindings have this option:

```
<div class="page-host">
  <!-- ko router: { cacheViews: false }--> <!-- /ko -->
</div>
```

You can see an example of this in the `cp6-cache` branch. If you open the console, you can see that the attaching and binding events are no longer being raised when revisiting the list or edit pages. You can also see, with a debugger breakpoint, that the viewmodels are only being constructed the first time.

When working with cached views, extra caution is required. As the module is a singleton and is only constructed once, the `activate` method is responsible for setting up data or clearing old data out. For example, previously, the edit page only set its `contact` property to a new instance during the construction. The `activate` method needs to reset the contact if the page is being loaded in a new entry mode (without an ID):

```
self.activate = function(id) {
  //Id is only present when editing
  if (id) {
    return dataService.getContact(id).then(self.contact);
  }
  else
  self.contact(new Contact());
};
```

If this isn't done, users will not see an empty form if they tried to create a contact after creating or editing a previous one.

Even if the `cacheViews` property is set to `true`, Durandal will not cache a DOM view if the model instance has changed. In the `cp6-cache2` branch, the constructor is returned from the list page, and you can see that a new instance is constructed and attached to the DOM despite `cacheViews` being set.

# Transitions

Durandal's `router` and `compose` bindings have a hook that allows the composed view to transition with an animation. To use it, provide a value to the `transition` property on the binding:

```
<!-- ko router: {
  cacheViews: false,
  transition: 'entrance'
}--> <!-- /ko -->
```

The `entrance` transition is provided by default; it fades the current view out and fades in the next view with a small slide effect. You can see it in the `cp6-entrance` branch. Note that for this animation to work, the composition needs to occur in an element with the CSS `position: relative` property, as the animation uses absolute positioning.

The `durandal/composition` module also has a `defaultTransitionName` property that will use the supplied transition for all compositions that do not specify their own transitions.

To create your own transition, you need a module that returns a function that Durandal can call in order to run the transition. The transition function will receive the composition settings and needs to return a promise for its completion. There are a lot of values on the settings object but the two that are most useful are `activeView`, which is the view being transition out, and `child`, which is the view being transitioned to.

Here is an example of a custom transition that uses the jQuery UI's slide effects. It assumes that jQueryUI has already been set up in RequireJS:

```
define(['durandal/system', 'jquery', 'jquery-ui'], function(system, $)
{

  var outDuration = 400,
  outDirection = 'down'
  inDuration = 400,
  inDirection = 'up',
  easing = 'swing';
```

```
    return function slideAnimation(settings) {

        var currentView = settings.activeView,
        newView = settings.child;

        return system.defer(function(defer) {
            function endTransition() {
                defer.resolve();
            }

            function slideIn() {
                $(newView).show('slide', { direction: inDirection, easing:
                    easing }, inDuration, endTransition);
            }

            if (currentView) {
                $(currentView).hide('slide', { direction: outDirection,
                    easing: easing }, outDuration, newView ? slideIn :
                    endTransition);
            } else {
                $(newView).show();
                endTransition();
            }

        }).promise();
    };
});
```

The module returns the animation function, which itself returns a promise for the animation. The animation function pulls out the current and next view and then sets up callbacks in order to end the view and slide in the new view with jQuery. The `if` block at the end ensures that the current view is only acted upon when it exists. If it doesn't, then no animation is created (as there is nothing to slide out), and the view is just shown.

By default, Durandal looks for transitions by appending `'transitions/'` to their name in order to get a RequireJS path. This is why the standard Durandal RequireJS configuration has a transitions path defined. You can map the path in RequireJS to another folder if you want to keep transitions somewhere else—such as your `app` folder—or you can override the composition module's `convertTransitionToModuleId` function to provide your own lookup logic.

This example can be seen in the `cp6-transition` branch. This branch uses a RequireJS path for a `transitions` folder in the `app` directory, which contains the preceding slide animation.

# The templated mode

In the previous chapter, we covered widgets, which offer us the ability to override sections of the composed element with `data-part` attributes. This feature is also available in viewmodel composition using the binding `mode: 'templated'` option.

The example widget that was used was a bit contrived, as the list of contacts isn't really a reusable widget. A more common technique with lists, especially with complex items, is to create a module for the list item and compose it with a `foreach` binding.

Separating complex list items from the page they are shown in keeps properties and methods specific to the list item that is not on the page. This is the same modularization logic that drives the separation of viewmodels and modules. It lets the page viewmodel focus more on the actions the page takes as a whole and lets the item focus on itself. The contact list items aren't complex enough to warrant this, but I'm sure you can imagine such a case.

Replacing the contact list widget with a `compose/foreach` binding is simple:

```
<ul class="list-unstyled" data-bind="foreach: displayContacts">
  <li data-bind="compose: $data"></li>

</ul>
```

This allows the item itself to be moved into its own file, which is `listItem.html`:

```
<h3 data-bind="with: contact">
  <span data-bind="text: displayName"></span>
  <small data-bind="text: phoneNumber" data-part="phone"></small>
  <div class="inline" data-part="btn-container">
    <button class="btn btn-sm btn-default" data-part="edit-btn"
      data-bind="click: edit">Edit</button>
  </div>
</h3>
```

This is the same template that was used previously, minus the delete button. The viewmodel for the list item is simple, containing just a `contact` object and an `edit` function:

```
define(['knockout', 'plugins/router'], function(ko, router) {
  return function ListItem(contact) {
    var self = this;

    self.contact = contact;
```

```
      self.edit = function() {
        router.navigate('contacts/' + self.contact.id());
      };
    };
  });
```

The last thing to do is construct the list item on the list page instead of just using the bare contact model:

```
self.activate = function() {
  return dataService.getContacts()
  .then(function(contacts) {
    var listItems = contacts.map(function(contact) {
      return new ListItem(contact);
    })
    self.contacts(listItems);
  });;
};
```

You can see this example in the cp6-list-item branch. This is just the setup, though; what we are really after is overriding the list item view with data-part attributes. Data-part overriding works the same way with compositions as it works with widgets:

```
<ul class="list-unstyled" data-bind="foreach: displayContacts">
  <li data-bind="compose: { model: $data, mode: 'templated' }">
    <div data-part="btn-container" class="inline">
      <button class="btn btn-sm btn-default" data-bind="click:
        edit">Edit</button>
      <button data-bind="click: $root.deleteContact" class="btn
        btn-sm btn-danger">Delete</button>
    </div>
  </li>
</ul>
```

Here, the entire btn-container element is being overridden so that a delete button can be added. Remember, the scope of data-part attributes is the view they will be placed into, which is listItem in this case. The edit function is already in this scope, but the deleteContact function is in the parent of listItem, which can be accessed using the $root property of the templated elements.

This example can be seen in the cp6-template-compose branch.

# Child routers

Another common scenario is the need to support routes within routes; this is sometimes called **nested** or **child** routes. For example, you might have multiple pages under the parent /about route that are represented by the /about/author and /about/publisher URLs, which are displayed as different subsections of the main /about page.

To do this, the parent route has to capture child routes. It can do this with a splat route or with the hasChildRoutes property:

```
router.map([
  { route: 'about', moduleId: 'about/index', title: 'About', nav:
    true, hasChildRoutes: true }
  //OR
  { route: 'about*children', moduleId: 'about/index', title:
    'About', nav: true }
]);
```

Either way is fine, but note that the about*children splat route requires at least one character after the asterisk (*); the about* route will not capture the children properly. Personally, I think the hasChildRoutes property has a clearer intention.

Next, the viewmodel that exposes child routes creates a child router:

```
define(['plugins/router'], function(router) {
  var childRouter = router.createChildRouter()
  .makeRelative({
    moduleId: 'about',
    fromParent: true
  }).map([
  { route: ['author', ''], moduleId: 'author', title: 'Author',
    nav: true },
  { route: 'publisher', moduleId: 'publisher', title: 'Publisher',
    nav: true }
  ]).buildNavigationModel();

  return {
    router:childRouter
  };
});
```

The createChildRouter function returns the child router of the root router. You can only have one root router, but it can have any number of children, and children routers can have children routers as well.

The `makeRelative` function takes an optional object. The `moduleId` option instructs all the modules of children routes to be prefixed with the supplied module, essentially making the routes relative to a folder. This is not required, but it keeps the routes shorter. The `fromParent` option causes children routes to inherit their parent's URL from the `route` property.

Finally, the module exposes `childRouter` as the router so that its view can bind to it using the same syntax that was used by the shell. This is the view for the `about` parent page:

```
<h1>About</h1>
//Text removed for clarity
<ul class="nav nav-tabs" role="tablist" data-bind="foreach:
  router.navigationModel">
  <li data-bind="css: { active: isActive }">
    <a class="" data-bind="attr: { href: hash }, text: title"></a>
  </li>
</ul>
<div class="page-sub-host">
  <!-- ko router: { cacheViews: false }--> <!-- /ko -->
</div>
```

This example can be seen in the `cp6-child-router` branch. The about page and its child routes are in the `app/about` folder, and the route has been added to the navigation bar.

# Dynamic child routes

When creating child routes for a parent route with a parameter, such as `/contacts/23/bio`, additional configuration is required in order to allow the child routes to be relative to the `/contacts/:id` dynamic parent. To see an example of this, we are going to add a biography and location section to our contact pages.

The contact edit route needs to indicate that it has child routes. The same options are available, but there is a caveat for splat routes—you must specify a `hash` manually:

```
{ route: 'contacts/:id', moduleId: 'contacts/edit', title:
  'Contact Details', nav: false, hasChildRoutes: true },
//OR
{ route: 'contacts/:id*children', moduleId: 'contacts/edit',
  title: 'Contact Details', nav: false, hash: 'contacts/:id' },
```

The children routers will not be able to create a proper URL from a splat route if the hash is not specified manually. This does not need to be done if you're using the `hasChildRoutes` flag.

The child router definition is almost identical, except for the `dynamicHash` property:

```
var childRouter = router.createChildRouter()
.makeRelative({
  moduleId: 'contacts/edit',
  fromParent: true,
  dynamicHash: ':id'
}).map([
    { route: ['details', ''], moduleId: 'details', title: 'Details',
      nav: true },
    { route: 'bio', moduleId: 'bio', title: 'Biography', nav: true
      },
    { route: 'location', moduleId: 'location', title: 'Location',
      nav: true }
]).buildNavigationModel();
```

The `dynamicHash` property controls how the URLs for child routes are created, as they need to include the `route` parameter. That's all it takes, though! After this, the routes can be used on the parameterized URL.

You can see an example of this in the `cp6-dynamic-child-routes` branch. The edit page's child routes have been placed for organization in the `contacts/edit` folder. Also, the biography and location pages just contain dummy text.

# Custom modal dialogs

In Durandal, a dialog context is the viewmodel that controls a modal dialog. It has a method used to add the modal dialog host, which is the DOM node inside which the modal content will be placed.

Durandal offers two modal dialogs out of the box: message boxes and the default context. The message box that Durandal offers adds some simple DOM elements to the default context and is very useful in order to show short messages to the user. The default dialog context can host any composable module, including message boxes. If you want to use your own dialog box, such as the one included in Twitter Bootstrap, it is possible to add it as a dialog context.

A dialog context is an object that can create a dialog in the DOM to which the composition can add content. A custom context uses the following APIs:

- `addHost(dialog)`: This function is responsible for creating the dialog itself, by adding it to the DOM. It must assign the `dialog.host` property on the parameter to this DOM node, which will be used by composition as the parent for the composing module.

- `removeHost(dialog)`: This function removes the DOM for the dialog and performs any cleanup.

- `compositionComplete(child, parent, context)`: This is a composition hook that the context can use to perform any setup. To get the `dialog` object (the parameter from the other two functions), call `dialog.getDialog(context.model)`.

Custom dialog contexts are useful when you have different needs for modal windows. The Twitter Bootstrap dialog, for example, uses the same responsive CSS system that the rest of the Bootstrap framework uses, making it perfect for dialogs that need to be usable on desktops and phones. You might also want some of your dialogs to be displayed in a circular pop up in order to differentiate them from other modals your application is using.

Working with custom dialogs is done using the `dialog` module, which is injected using `'plugins/dialog'`. You can add a custom dialog context with the `dialog.addContext` function, which takes a context that matches the preceding API. The first parameter is the name of the new context, and the second is the context object:

```
dialog.addContext('bootstrap', {
  addHost: function (dialogInstance) {
    //Create dialog, add to DOM
  },
  removeHost: function (dialogInstance) {
    //Remove dialog from DOM
  },
  compositionComplete: function (child, parent, context) {
    //Perform setup
  }
});
```

This setup needs to be done before the dialog can be used, so it is good to do it with any app setup. In the upcoming example, this will be in the `common/extensions` module.

The actual setup logic for each of the context methods depends on the dialog you are adding. This is what the Bootstrap modal setup will look like:

```
addHost: function (dialogInstance) {
  var body = $('body'),
  host = $('<div class="modal fade"><div class="modal-dialog"><div
class="modal-content"></div></div></div>');
  host.appendTo(body);
  dialogInstance.host = host.find('.modal-content').get(0);
  dialogInstance.modalHost = host;
}
```

Unlike the Durandal modal, where the content container and the dialog element are the same, the Bootstrap modal expects the content container to be inside the dialog element. The content's DOM element is placed in the `dialogInstance.host` property, which Durandal will use to compose the module. The outer modal element is stored in the `modalHost` property, which will only be used by functions on our custom Bootstrap context:

```
compositionComplete: function (child, parent, context) {
  var dialogInstance = dialog.getDialog(context.model),
  $child = $(child);
  $(dialogInstance.modalHost).modal({ backdrop: 'static',
    keyboard: false, show: true });

  //Setting a short timeout is need in IE8, otherwise we could do
    this straight away
  setTimeout(function () {
    $child.find('.autofocus').first().focus();
  }, 1);

  if ($child.hasClass('autoclose') || context.model.autoclose) {
    $(dialogInstance.blockout).click(function () {
      dialogInstance.close();
    });
  }
}
```

This is where the actual Bootstrap `$.modal()` code is run from, as the sizing and placement of the modal will need to have a fully composed module that already exists. It uses the `modalHost` property and not the `host` property, as Bootstrap is expecting the modal container. Additionally, the handler is set up to support the standard Durandal autofocus and autoclose classes:

```
removeHost: function (dialogInstance) {
  $(dialogInstance.modalHost).modal('hide');''''''
}
```

The `removeHost` function takes the steps that are required to hide the modal and the backdrop.

Finally, we use this new modal by specifying the context parameter on `dialog.show` in the edit contact viewmodel:

```
self.show = function() {
  return dialog.show(self, null, ''bootstrap'');
};
```

If you look in the `cp6-bootstrap-dialog` branch, this context will be added. The modal dialog from *Chapter 5, Durandal – the Knockout Framework,* that opens when the **Add Contact** button on the list page is pressed has been restored. You can see that this new dialog has the Bootstrap sliding entrance animation, and the content is responsive.

There is another method that can be used to show custom dialogs. The `addContext` method automatically creates a helper method using the context name. For the Bootstrap context, the method is `dialog.showBootrap`:

```
self.show = function() {
  return dialog.showBootstrap(self);
};
```

You can see this example in the `cp6-bootstrap-dialog2` branch.

# Replacing the default context

Having multiple dialog contexts is certainly useful, but if you are adding a custom dialog context, chances are you want it to be the default dialog context. Having a Bootstrap modal dialog is great, but the standard message boxes are still using the nonresponse Durandal context. To change this, just replace the `dialog.show` method with one that specifies your context when one isn't explicitly provided:

```
var oldShow = dialog.show;
dialog.show = function(obj, data, context) {
  return oldShow.call(dialog, obj, data, context || 'bootstrap');
};
```

This will cause all regular calls to the dialog module to use this context without affecting the ability of the code to manually control which dialog context is used for special scenarios:

```
//Shows using the Bootstrap dialog
app.showMessage('Are you sure you want to delete ' + contact.
displayName() + '?', 'Delete Contact?', ['No', 'Yes']);
//Shows using the Bootstrap dialog
self.show = function() {
  return dialog.show(self);
};
//Uses the bubble context, equivalent to calling dialog.showBubble();
self.show = function() {
  return dialog.show(self, null, 'bubble');
};
```

In the `cp6-bootstrap-dailog3` branch, you can see that the delete confirmation message box as well as the add contact modal uses the Bootstrap dialog context.

If you still need access to the default context, consider adding a conventional helper to the dialog object, such as `dialog.showDefault` or `dialog.showOld`:

```
var oldShow = dialog.show;
dialog.show = function(obj, data, context) {
  return oldShow.call(dialog, obj, data, context || 'bootstrap');
};
dialog.showDefault = oldShow;
```

# Using activators

The activation life cycle is automatically used by the router, but sometimes, you want to use it without tying the work to the URL, which turns out to be quite easy. An activator is just a computed observable whose write function enforces the life cycle. An activator can be created by calling `activator.create()` using the `durandal/activator` module.

For this example, we are going to add an inline *quick edit* to the list page that will allow contacts to be edited without navigating to another page. It will leverage the existing edit page viewmodel with some minor changes, as it already has a `canDeactivate` method that prompts the user with a confirmation modal when unsaved changes are present. The list page activator will hook into the same logic automatically.

This example is in the `cp6-activator` branch. You might want to play with it a bit before we go into how it works. Just use the quick edit button on the list page, and the contact will be loaded into an edit form just below the search box.

The list page needs an activator and a function to set the activator:

```
self.editContact = activator.create();
self.quickEdit = function(listItem) {
  self.editContact(new ContactVM(listItem.contact, function() {
    self.editContact(null);
  }));
};
```

The `quickEdit` function, which will be bound to a button on the list item, sets the `editContact` activator to a new instance of the edit page viewmodel. It provides the contact-to-edit to the new viewmodel and a callback to clear the `editContact` object. The HTML just needs a button to call it:

```
<ul class="list-unstyled" data-bind="foreach: displayContacts">
  <li data-bind="compose: { model: $data, mode: 'templated' }">
```

```
      <div data-part="btn-container" class="inline">
        <button class="btn btn-sm btn-default" data-bind="click:
          edit">Edit</button>
        <button class="btn btn-sm btn-default" data-bind="click:
          $root.quickEdit">Quick Edit</button>
        <button data-bind="click: $root.deleteContact" class="btn
          btn-sm btn-danger">Delete</button>
      </div>
    </li>
  </ul>
```

To use this, the edit page viewmodel will need to call the close callback—the second constructor parameter—when saving or canceling in a manner that is similar to how it handled closing the dialog:

```
function EditContactVm(initContact, closeCallback) {

  ///...

  self.close = function(result) {
    if (closeCallback) {
      closeCallback();
    } else if (dialog.getDialog(self)) {
      dialog.close(self, result);
    } else {
      router.navigate('''');
    }
  };
```

Actually, this is all we need in order to take advantage of the deactivation guard, which is already on the edit viewmodel. There is some additional logic that handles saving changes, but it isn't strictly related to the activator use. If you try to use quick edit, make some changes, hit **Cancel**, and you will be prompted. If you hit **No**, the item will not be deactivated. You will also be prompted if you try to use a different quick edit while unsaved changes are present. All of this guard logic is handled for you by virtue of editContact being an activator observable.

In addition to being writeable with the normal observable pattern by calling editContact(newValue), activators have an activateItem method. The first parameter to activateItem is newValue, and the second option is activationData, which allows you to send a property bag to the activate method of the new value being set. This will be used as editContact.activateItem(newValue, data).

This example, more than most examples in this book, is extremely contrived for the sake of brevity. Overloading the edit page viewmodel so that it is internally aware of being used in three different contexts is not a good design, and is not recommended for real-world use.

# Binding to plain JavaScript objects

The last part of Durandal that we are going to cover is the observable plugin, which allows data binding to use normal viewmodel properties as observable objects by converting them under the hood.

The observable plugin uses JavaScript getters and setters created with `defineProperty`, which is part of the ECMAScript 5 specification. Only modern browsers support this feature, so if your application needs to work in Internet Explorer 8, the observable plugin will not work.

Using the observable plugin removes one of the most common complaints from Knockout's syntax: the parentheses. All of the property access is executed using plain syntax, whether reading or assigning values:

```
function Contact() {
  var self = this;
  self.firstName = '';
  self.lastName = '';
  self.reset = function() {
    self.firstName = '';
    self.lastName = ''
  };
};

var viewmodel = new Contact();

//HTML
<input data-bind="value: firstName" />
<input data-bind="value: lastName" />
<button data-bind="click: reset">Reset</button>
```

Everything is converted into observables by the observable plugin during data binding. Knockout observables can still be created with `ko.observable`, but it should not be necessary.

This does have an impact on all of your code, though, as using the parentheses to access properties will no longer work; they are not functions anymore! Using the observable plugin means a total conversion of your application code.

# Observable plugin setup

Using the observable plugin, like any plugin, requires it to be installed before the `app.start` call:

```
app.configurePlugins({
  router:true,
  dialog: true,
  observable: true
});
app.start().then(function () {
  app.setRoot('shell/shell');
});
```

If you need to use the plugin manually, it is required into a module with `plugins/observable`.

# Subscribing and extending

When you are no longer creating observables manually, you will have to use the observable plugin to get access to the underlying observable to set up subscriptions or add extenders. This can be done by calling the observable module as a function with `observable(object, 'property')`. The observable module is injected with `'plugins/observable'`:

```
function Contact() {
  //Same as before

  observable(self, 'firstName').subscribe(function(value){
    console.log('First name changed.');
  });

  observable(self, 'firstName').extend({
    rateLimit: {
      timeout: 100,
      method: 'notifyWhenChangesStop'
    }
  });
};
```

This can be done at any time, even if the property hasn't yet been converted into an observable, as calling the observable module will convert the property immediately.

# Computed observables

Computed observables are created using `observable.defineProperty`:

```
observable.defineProperty(self, 'displayName', function() {
  var nickname = self.nickname || '';
  if (nickname.length > 0) {
    return nickname;
  } else if ((self.firstName || '').length > 0) {
    return self.firstName + ' ' + self.lastName;
  } else {
    return 'New Contact';
  }
});
```

The `defineProperty` method also returns the underlying computed observables so that it can be extended or subscribed to.

There is a caveat with computed observables, though. If anything tries to access the computed value before its dependencies have been converted into observables, then the computed value will not be able to register these dependencies; its value will never update:

```
return function Contact(init) {
  var self = this;

  self.id = 0;
  self.firstName = '';
  self.lastName = '';
  self.nickname = '';
  self.phoneNumber = '';

  observable.defineProperty(self, 'displayName', function() {
    var nickname = self.nickname || '';
    if (nickname.length > 0)
    return nickname;
    else if ((self.firstName || '').length > 0)
    return self.firstName + ' ' + self.lastName;
    else
    return 'New Contact';
  });

  //This will break the display name property
  var name = self.displayName;
}
```

To stop this from happening, the dependencies `firstName`, `lastName`, and `nickname` need to be made observables manually. This can be done by calling `convertObject` on the observable module:

```
observable.convertObject(self);
observable.defineProperty(self, 'displayName', function() {
  //
});
```

This ensures that the first time `displayName` is accessed, it reads observable properties and not normal properties.

Because this *bug* can be difficult to track down when it happens, it can be a good practice to always call `convertObject` in viewmodel constructors. It does not incur any performance penalty, as it's the same method the observable plugin uses when it gets to data binding. If you need finer-grained control over conversion, properties can be converted one at a time using `observable.convertProperty(object, 'propertyName')`.

# Promises

In addition to treating normal JavaScript properties as observables, the observables plugin also allows promises to be bound against by converting the property into an observable and setting a callback to update it when the promise is resolved:

```
self.contacts = dataService.getContacts()
.then(function(contacts) {
  return contacts.map(function(contact) {
    return new ListItem(contact);
  });
});
```

After being converted into an observable, the contacts array can still be bound against normally. In fact, making this change requires no HTML changes in the sample code.

# Sample

You can see an example of all of these binding methods in the `cp6-observable` branch. All of the code has been converted to using plain JavaScript properties with the observable plugin.

The parentheses have been removed from all of the application code, including the mock data service. It should be a bit easier to read now.

On the list viewmodel, the preceding contacts' promise example is used, which replaces the `activate` method. The `displayContacts` computed value is created with the observable plugin and still has the `rateLimit` extender applied.

The `Contact` model uses the `convertObject` method to manually convert to observables, as the dirty flag on `state` will try to read the `displayName` computed value.

The only changes on the edit page are the removal of parentheses.

# Summary

Durandal aims to compliment Knockout's MVVM philosophy by providing a view-viewmodel-centric framework that focuses on composition. If you love Knockout (and you should; you're reading this book, after all!), you should hopefully see Durandal as a natural extension. The tools Durandal provides go a long way in simplifying the development of SPAs.

In the next chapter, we will be leaving Durandal and deep diving into Knockout's inner workings.

# 7
# Best Practices

Up until now, all the coding recommendations have been interspersed with Knockout techniques as they were introduced. In order to go into more detail about these patterns and why they are useful as well as to provide a consolidated reference, we are going to review them in this chapter. As JavaScript is a very flexible language, enjoys one of the largest online developer communities, and is in use at all levels of development on the hobbyist-enterprise spectrum, it is difficult to talk about good or useful patterns without becoming opinionated. These practices should be taken as advice and shouldn't be considered dogma. Many of these recommendations are applicable to programming in general and not just Knockout development.

## Sticking to MVVM

Knockout was designed with the **Model-View-ViewModel** (**MVVM**) pattern in mind. While it is possible to develop applications using Knockout and other design patterns, sticking to MVVM will produce a natural alignment between Knockout and your own code.

## The view and the viewmodel

The separation of concerns is the key here. Don't introduce view concepts such as DOM elements or CSS classes into your viewmodel; these belong in the HTML. Limit or avoid business logic and inline binding functions in your view; these belong as properties or functions in your viewmodel. Keeping these two separated makes it possible for the work to be divided and parallelized, allows the viewmodel to be reusable, and makes it possible to unit test the viewmodel.

# Cluttering the viewmodel

Animation handlers are a good example of view logic that often ends up in the viewmodel. The `foreach` binding handler has several postprocessing hooks (such as `afteradd`, `afterrender`, and `beforeremove`) that are intended to allow animations to be used. It might seem natural to use viewmodel functions, as they are specified in a binding, which normally takes viewmodel properties:

```
<div data-bind='template: { foreach: planetsToShow,
                            beforeRemove: hidePlanetElement,
                            afterAdd: showPlanetElement }'>
    <div data-bind='attr: { "class": "planet " + type }, text:
name'></div>
</div>


var PlanetsModel = function() {
    //Viewmodel properties
    this.planets = ko.observableArray();

    // Animation callbacks for the planets list
    this.showPlanetElement = function(elem) {
        if (elem.nodeType === 1) {
$(elem).hide().slideDown() ;
}
    }
    this.hidePlanetElement = function(elem) {
        if (elem.nodeType === 1) {
$(elem).slideUp(function() { $(elem).remove(); });
}
    }
};
```

Unfortunately, this tightly couples the viewmodel to the view and makes both the viewmodel and the animation less reusable. A better solution would be to store the animations somewhere globally accessible, such as `ko.animations`, and reference them in the binding:

```
<div data-bind='template: { foreach: planetsToShow,
                            beforeRemove: ko.animations.slideHide,
                            afterAdd: ko.animations.slideShow }'>
    <div data-bind='attr: { "class": "planet " + type }, text:
name'></div>
</div>

ko.animations = {};
```

```
ko.animations.slideShow = function(elem) {
    if (elem.nodeType === 1) {
$(elem).hide().slideDown();
}
};
ko.animations.slideHide =  function(elem) {
    if (elem.nodeType === 1) {
$(elem).slideUp(function() { $(elem).remove(); });
    }
};

var PlanetsModel = function() {
    //Viewmodel properties
    this.planets = ko.observableArray();
};
```

Now, the same animations can be reused in other lists, and the viewmodel doesn't contain logic that controls the DOM.

# Cluttering the view

While keeping the viewmodel agnostic of the view tends to be very clear cut (don't reference HTML types), keeping inline code out of the view tends to merit more consideration. This is partially because logic related to the presentation might belong in the view, or at least a binding handler, and partially because there is a balancing act when many small, one-off properties are required.

An example of inline logic that does not belong in the view is a button-disabling expression:

```
<button data-bind="disable: items().length > 3, click:
submitOrder">Submit</button>
```

Consider the case where this value needs to change: do you really want to hunt through the HTML for the rule that controls this? What about when this value is variable and is determined by other factors? This should absolutely be canSubmit (or similarly named) that is computed in the viewmodel, because the maximum number of items is business logic, which is not the view's domain.

A less clear-cut example is a warning display based on similar logic. Let's say disabling the button isn't enough of a visual cue, and you also want the button to turn red:

```
<form data-bind="submit: submitOrder, css: { 'invalid-form': items().
length > maxItems }">
    //Irrelevant form code...
</form>
```

This isn't a perfect example, and you might want to add an `overMaxItemLimit` computed to your viewmodel anyway; and it does not directly express the business logic either. *If the form has too many items, highlight the form* is presentation logic, and if you have enough of these one-off computed properties, which just contain a simple expression against a single observable, your viewmodel will get cluttered quickly. In cases like these, forcing the viewmodel to represent this logic might not offer any value, and you should use discretion when deciding where to put it.

# Using service modules

Viewmodels should not contain all of your application code even in small applications. When possible, code should be broken out into non-viewmodel modules that encapsulate the work and can be reused. These modules are often called services.

For example, a viewmodel that gets data from the server doesn't need to know how that operation is handled, whether it uses jQuery's AJAX method, a websocket, or some other retrieval method. Putting this logic into a data service module not only makes it reusable by other viewmodels, it makes unit testing easier by limiting the scope of each object to its own work. The driving philosophy here is the single responsibility principle.

# Creating small modules

Creating smaller modules makes unit testing simpler and reduces the effort required to understand the code for others who have to read it. When deciding whether or not to add functionalities to a module or split it off into a new one, keep the single responsibility principle in mind.

This is a bit of a balancing act. If you have a RESTful API for your JavaScript application, then creating modules to abstract away the individual URLs by providing methods for them is a good idea. Having a single dataService module that contains all of the URLs for the whole application, though, will result in a very large module in even medium-sized applications. On the other hand, having a service module for each individual route will produce an even larger number of files. This will make unit testing and maintenance harder, it won't make it easier. The best course is to group the routes into modules by functionality. In the case of REST URLs, grouping them by resource produces a very natural organization.

# Writing unit tests

If you follow all the previous recommendations, then your code will be in a good position to be unit tested. The primary consideration while writing unit testable code is mockability: code whose external dependencies are loosely coupled. Loosely coupled dependencies can be replaced in a unit test with a fake, stub, mock, spy, or other form of replacement whose behavior can be controlled by the test. This challenge is solved by keeping DOM and binding the code out of your viewmodel, keeping the modules small and avoiding tight coupling to other viewmodels through practices such as dependency injection.

There are several frameworks that are available for unit testing in JavaScript, and they all offer similar benefits and workflows. The important thing is not what tools you use to unit test, only that you write unit tests. The value of unit testing really can't be overstated. It is even more important in dynamic languages such as JavaScript that do not offer compile-time checking.

# Singleton versus instance

When you have a viewmodel that is actually used multiple times, such as the one backing a `foreach` loop, using an instance is the only option. When there is only one instance of the viewmodel, such as the one backing an entry form or a page in an SPA, the choice might not be as simple.

A good rule of thumb is to think about the lifetime of the object. If the object's lifetime doesn't end, such as the viewmodel for an ever-present navigation bar, using a singleton is appropriate. If the object's lifetime is short, such as a page viewmodel in an SPA, then using a singleton means that the object cannot be garbage collected even after it is no longer being actively used. In this situation, a disposable instance is recommended.

Another rule of thumb is to consider whether or not it has an internal state. Without an internal state that needs to be managed, there is little danger that multiple uses of the object or its methods will result in errors. If an object has no internal state, such as a service that abstracts AJAX requests or cookie access, a singleton is appropriate even if the object has a limited lifetime. This is not true for a viewmodel whose state is important, such as one backing an entry form; this is because with each use, it should have a fresh state. The need for a fresh state is there even if the object has a long lifetime, such as the login viewmodel in a navigation bar. Reconstructing the viewmodel after a logout will ensure that no information from a previous use remains.

# Calling ko.applyBindings once (per root)

I can't tell you how many times I've come across questions on Stack Overflow regarding problems that come from developers calling `ko.applyBindings` multiple times, thinking that it is responsible for syncing the DOM and the observable data. This is more of a *warning* than a *best practice*, but I would feel remiss if I left it out entirely. For any given root element in your HTML, you should have one call to `ko.applyBindings` at most.

# Performance concerns

Knockout's performance has improved several times since its initial release, but it is still possible to encounter issues in apps with a large number of operations or objects. While some decrease in performance should be expected as the work being done increases, there are ways to ease the burden on the CPU.

# Observable loops

Changing observable arrays inside loops causes them to publish change notifications multiple times. The cost of these changes is proportional to the size of the array. You might need to add several items to an array and use a loop to do this:

```
var contacts = ko.observableArray();
for (var i = 0, j = newContacts.length; i < j; i++) {
    contacts.push(new Contact(newContacts[i]);
}
```

The problem here is that push gets called multiple times, which causes the array to send out multiple change notifications. It's much easier for the subscribers of the array if all of the changes are sent at once. This can be done by collecting all of the changes in the loop and then applying them to the observable array at the end with push.apply:

```
var contacts = ko.observableArray();
for (var i = 0, j = newContacts.length, newItems = []; i < j; i++) {
    newItems.push(new Contact(newContacts[i]);
}
contacts.push.apply(contacts, newItems);
```

The preceding method ensures that only a single call to valueHasMutated happens for the observable array. A popular solution to this common problem is to add this into a function on the `observableArray.fn` object, making it available to all observable arrays:

```
ko.observableArray.fn.pushAll = function (items) {
    this.push.apply(this, items);
};
```

The following method can be used to add an array of items:

```
var contacts = ko.observableArray();
for (var i = 0, j = newContacts.length, newItems = []; i < j; i++) {
    newItems.push(new Contact(newContacts[i]);
}

contacts.pushAll(newitems);
```

# Limit active bindings

A large number of bindings, especially those that register event handlers such as value and click can quickly lead to poor browser performance. Managing this takes careful consideration about how to best reduce the number of changes that need to happen simultaneously.

One method is to use control flow bindings to remove bound sections that are not required. Limiting the amount of content on the screen helps performance and also has the incidental benefit of reducing the clutter that users need to parse. Techniques such as pagination can be used for more than just long lists, such as breaking up a long form or activity into several screens. Of course, this method is limited to activities that can be broken up.

A more broadly applicable method is to use delegated events, which are otherwise known as **unobtrusive event handlers**.

# Delegated events

Unobtrusive event handlers, such as jQuery's on, can use a single event handler to respond to events on any number of DOM elements that are inside the registered element. This is especially useful in large or recursive lists where registering a single event handler per element would be too expensive. Knockout provides two utility methods to connect these handlers with the appropriate data from the binding context in a manner that's similar to the how Knockout's click binding provides the context as the first parameter:

- ko.dataFor (element): This returns the data that is available to the element
- ko.contextFor (element): This returns the binding context for the element (includes binding context properties such as $parent and $root)

This can be combined with a binding handler that provides the event delegation:

```
ko.bindingHandlers.on = {
    init: function(element, valueAccessor, allBindings, viewModel,
bindingContext) {
        var options = valueAccessor();
        var handler = function() {
            options.method.call(bindingContext.$rawData,
ko.dataFor(this));
        };

        $(element).on(options.event, options.selector, handler);

        ko.utils.domNodeDisposal.addDisposeCallback(element, function()
{
            $(element).off(options.event, options.selector, handler);
        });
    }
};
```

```
<ul class="list-unstyled" data-bind="foreach: displayContacts, on: {
event: 'click', selector: '.remove-btn', method: deleteContact }">
  <li data-bind="compose: { model: $data, mode: 'templated' }">
  <div data-part="btn-container" class="inline">
    <button class="btn btn-sm btn-default"  data-bind="click:
edit">Edit</button>
    <button class="btn btn-sm btn-danger remove-btn">Delete</button>
  </div>
  </li>
</ul>
```

The preceding example can be seen in the cp7-unobtrusive branch.

The preceding technique is not required everywhere, but when dealing with large numbers of handlers, it can lead to a noticeable impact on performance.

# Summary

Again, these are guidelines and not rules, and some of them are opinions that will lead to disagreement among coworkers. Sometimes, breaking the pattern produces cleaner and clearer code and is the only way to get something working while sometimes, breaking the pattern is the only way to compromise with colleagues. If it's getting in your way without giving you any benefits, don't do it. There is no one right way to develop software.

The next chapter will cover some popular Knockout plugins maintained by the community.

# 8
# Plugins and Other Knockout Libraries

A big part of effectively working in any area of software is to be familiar with the tools used by the community. It is often better to rely on existing libraries and plugins that have been used and tested in the real world than try to reinvent the wheel on each new project. In this chapter, we will be looking at some of the most popular Knockout plugins:

- Knockout Validation
- Knockout Mapping
- Knockout Kendo
- KoGrid
- Knockout Bootstrap
- Knockout Switch-Case
- Knockout Projections
- Knockout-ES5

## Knockout Validation

The validation of user input is a common enough task that nearly every web application will have at least some need for. By far the most popular Knockout plugin, with 50 percent more stars on GitHub than the next Knockout related project, Knockout Validation creates several extenders and binding handlers that are designed to simplify HTML form validation.

The use of the plugin starts with extenders that apply validation logic to observables without replacing them:

```
var requiredValue = ko.observable().extend({ required: true });
var multipleValidationValue = ko.observable().extend({
                    required: true,
                    minLength: 3,
                    pattern: {
                          message: 'Hey this doesnt match my pattern',
                          params: '^[A-Z0-9].$'
                    }
              });
```

Binding against validation-extended values is done with the normal `value` binding:

```
<input data-bind="value: requiredValue" />
```

Knockout Validation modifies the standard value and checked bindings so that they display invalid value warnings. The default display behavior will place a span element that contains any errors after the value-bound input element. The error message span will be hidden when the value is valid and contain the error message text when invalid.

This automatic error insertion can be disabled if you want to manually place the validation message in the view. To do this, use the `validationMessage` binding, which has the same behavior as the inserted span.

## Default validation rules

Knockout Validation provides several validation extenders by default, which it calls **rules**. Like normal extenders, multiple validation rules can be passed in order to extend in a single call, or they can be chained:

```
var myObj = ko.observable().extend({ required: true });
var myObj = ko.observable().extend({ number: true, min: 10, max: 30
});
var myObj = ko.observable().extend({ number: true})
    .extend({ min: 10, max: 30 });
```

The default rules cover most of the standard cases for checking values, including—but not limited to—numerical min and max, string length min and max, regex patterns, dates, and value equality.

# Configuring validation options

Knockout Validation's behavior is very configurable. Some of the more useful options include:

- `insertMessages` (default: `true`): If true, a `span` will be inserted after an input that is bound to a validated observable.

- `errorElementClass` (default: `validationElement`): This is a class that is applied to elements when validated observables are invalid.

- `messagesOnModified` (default: `true`): If true, validation messages will not get displayed until the validated value has been modified so that they are hidden until a user interacts with the form.

- `messageTemplate` (default: `null`): This is an ID of a script element that will be used as the validation message template instead of inserting the message into a span.

Configuration options can be set globally by passing an object to `ko.validation.init`:

```
ko.validation.init({
    insertMessages: false,
    errorElementClass: 'text-danger'
});
```

Options can also be set contextually using the `validationOption` binding (see the next section) or by passing a configuration object to `ko.applyBindingsWithValidation`:

```
ko.applyBindingsWithValidation(viewModel, rootNode, {
    insertMessages: false,
    errorElementClass: 'text-danger'
});
```

# Validation binding handlers

Knockout Validation adds a few binding handlers to assist in displaying validation errors.

The `validationMessage` binding displays the error message for validated observables when they are invalid. When the value is valid, the element is hidden:

```
<div>
    <input type="text" data-bind="value: someValue"/>
    <p data-bind="validationMessage: someValue"></p>
</div>
```

The `validationElement` binding is useful for applying attributes and classes to elements. It sets the title attribute to the validation message, which is useful for showing tooltips, and it sets `errorElementClass` (`validationElement` by default) as the element's class attribute when the `decorateElement` configuration option is true:

```
<div>
    <label data-bind="validationElement: someValue">
      <input type="text" data-bind="value: someValue"/>
    </label>
</div>
```

The `validationOptions` binding is similar to a control flow binding in that it applies the specified configuration options to all descendant DOM nodes. It can take the same object format that the configuration options can take:

```
<div data-bind="validationOptions: { insertMessages: false } ">
    <input type="text" data-bind="value: someValue"/>
    <p data-bind="validationMessage: someValue"></p>
</div>
```

# Creating custom rules

Custom rules can be created both globally so that they can be reused by multiple extenders or inline for use in a single extender. Adding global validation rules is done by adding a rule object to the `ko.validation.rules` object. A rule has two components, which are the **validator function** and the **default message**:

```
ko.validation.rules['contains'] = {
    validator: function (val, substring) {
        return val.indexof(substring) !== -1;
    },
    message: 'The field must contain {0}'
};
```

The validator function receives two arguments: the value of the observable and the value passed to the validation extender. The validation extender can take any valid JavaScript value, including objects and functions.

Once a validation rule has been added, its extender is created with the following call:

```
ko.validation.registerExtenders();
```

It can then be used to extend observables:

```
var title = ko.observable().extend({ contains: 'Sr.' });
```

Inline validation rules work by passing the same validation rule object to the validation extender:

```
var title = ko.observable().extend({
    validation: {
        validator: function (val, substring) {
            return val.indexof(substring) !== -1;
        },
        message: 'The field must contain {0}',
        params: 'Sr.'
    }
});
```

When using inline validation rules, the second parameter to the `validator` function is defined with the `params` property of the validation rule.

 Knockout Validation is a large library with many features and options that have not been discussed in this section. The complete documentation for the Knockout Validation library can be found on its GitHub repository at `https://github.com/Knockout-Contrib/Knockout-Validation`.

# Knockout Mapping

The Knockout Mapping plugin is the answer to projects that want to bind against their server's AJAX responses without manually writing the JavaScript classes in order to convert them into observables. The mapping plugin will convert JavaScript objects or JSON strings into objects with observable properties:

```
var mappedViewmodel = ko.mapping.fromJS({
    name: 'Timothy Moran',
    age: 24
});
ko.applyBindings(mappedViewmodel);
```

For JSON, take a look at the following code:

```
var serverResponse = "{"name":"Timothy Moran","age":24}";
var mappedViewmodel = ko.mapping.fromJSON(serverResponse);
ko.applyBindings(mappedViewmodel);
```

The mapping plugin handles arrays by converting them into `observableArrays`. It also creates a copy of objects, allowing a complete object graph from the server to be converted into an observable object.

Updates against viewmodels created with the mapping plugin can be performed by passing the viewmodel as the second parameter to `fromJS` or `fromJSON`:

```
ko.mapping.fromJS(data, viewModel);
```

You can see a simple example of the mapping plugin in action in the `cp8-mapping` branch.

# Updating the viewmodel

The `fromJS` and `fromJSON` methods can also be used to update an entire viewmodel in order to handle future server update responses by passing the viewmodel as the third parameter:

```
ko.mapping.fromJS(data, {}, viewModel);
```

# Unmapping

Normally, when sending data back to the server, you would use `ko.toJS` or `ko.toJSON` to unwrap the viewmodel into an object with normal JavaScript properties instead of observables ones. Because the mapping plugin adds several properties to your viewmodel that are intended for internal use, `ko.toJS` will produce a cluttered copy. Instead, you can use `ko.mapping.toJS` and `ko.mapping.toJSON` to get an unwrapped viewmodel without the added mapping properties.

# Mapping options

To control how objects are created or updated by the mapping plugin, options can be passed in when a viewmodel is first created. The mapping plugin will use the options to build the viewmodel, and then store the options so that they can be used for all future updates:

```
var mapping = {
    // options
};

var vm = ko.mapping.fromJS(data, mapping);
```

# Using keys for array updates

The default behavior for updating arrays is to replace any elements that are not a perfect match with the new values. When working with arrays of objects, it is usually expected that the elements will have their values updated in place. To tell the mapping plugin how to determine that elements in the values to be updated are the same as the old values, a key can be defined:

```
var mapping = {
    people: {
        key: function(person) {
            return ko.unwrap(person.id);
        }
    }
};
var vm = ko.mapping.fromJS(data, mapping);
```

# Using create for the object construction

You can provide a callback for individual properties to control their creation. A common use case is to provide a constructor for the object:

```
var mapping = {
    people: {
        key: function(person) { /* same as before */ },
        create: function(options) {
            return new Person(options.data);
        }
    }
};
var vm = ko.mapping.fromJS(data, mapping);
```

# Controlling updates

Similar to creation, an update callback can be provided. The return value will be used as the property's value:

```
var mapping = {
    price: {
        update: function (options) {
            return parseMoney(options.data);
        }
    }
};
var vm = ko.mapping.fromJS(data, mapping);
```

# Choosing which properties get mapped

Mapping options can specify an array of property names that control various aspects of mapping:

- `ignore`: Mapping will not include these in the generated viewmodel.

- `copy`: Mapping will copy the values of these properties directly instead of converting them into observable properties.

- `observe`: If present, only the properties in this array will be converted into observable properties on the viewmodel. This is the inverse of the previous option.

- `include`: Normally when using `ko.mapping.toJS`, only properties that were originally in the mapping will be in the output. Any properties in the `include` array will also be copied into the output even if they weren't in the original viewmodel.

All of these arrays will be combined with the default values in the `ko.mapping.defaultOptions` object. The defaults are all empty by default, but they can be modified:

```
ko.mapping.defaultOptions().ignore = ["alwaysIgnoreThis"];
ko.mapping.defaultOptions().copy = ["alwaysCopyThis"];
```

# Challenges

The Knockout Mapping plugin is very useful in cases where server responses drive the work being done by the application. When the application needs to work with models, the mapping plugin will not be able to create the viewmodel before the models have been sent by the server. This happens commonly when filling out forms to create new models for the first time. The properties of a viewmodel are also only half the story; business logic will still need to be written for most viewmodels. It can be challenging to write functions or computed properties against properties that are populated by the mapping plugin, as they are not in the class that will be served as a reference. In very complex cases, the mapping logic for some objects might exceed the same logic for an object defined with normal JavaScript. While this can save time in medium-to-large applications with many server responses, it might not always be the best fit for a project.

Despite its popularity, it is no longer being maintained on GitHub. However, as of version 3.2, it still works with Knockout.

The documentation for the mapping plugin is on the official Knockout site at http://knockoutjs.com/documentation/plugins-mapping.html.

# Knockout Kendo

Kendo UI (http://www.telerik.com/kendo-ui) is a popular HTML5 widgets library of Telerik that offers a large selection of professional-looking controls. Knockout Kendo is a library of bindings, which allows Knockout viewmodels to use Kendo controls. Knockout Kendo has over 30 bindings, each with a variety of options, which is far too many to cover here. While Knockout Kendo is free, Kendo UI itself is not free and requires you to purchase a license in order to use it.

Most of the bindings are simple wrappers around the Kendo widgets, offering an API with a few surprises. For example, here is the **autocomplete** binding, which takes an array of options and an observable that binds the selection:

```
<input data-bind="kendoAutoComplete: { data: autocompleteOptions,
value: autocompleteValue }" /><br>
```

`DateTimePicker`, which creates two independent selection controls for the date and time, binds against a single observable `Date` object:

```
<input data-bind="kendoDateTimePicker: startDate" />
```

If you have used Kendo previously, you will be familiar with the available controls, and Knockout Kendo even has bindings for the non-free Professional UI widgets. You can see a few examples of Kendo controls in the `cp8-kendo` branch.

 You can find the complete documentation for Knockout Kendo on its GitHub site at http://rniemeyer.github.io/knockout-kendo/.

# KoGrid

KoGrid is a plugin that creates a binding that renders tabular data. As its GitHub page notes, it is "a direct knockout port of ng-grid which was originally inspired by KoGrid, which was inspired by SlickGrid." Its history might have been affected by the grandfather paradox.

In its most basic operation mode, KoGrid can bind against an array of objects, turning their properties into columns and their values into cells:

```
var vm = {
    people: ko.observableArray([{name: "Moroni", age: 50},
                                {name: "Tiancum", age: 43},
                                {name: "Jacob", age: 27},
                                {name: "Nephi", age: 29},
                                {name: "Enos", age: 34}])
    }
<div class="gridStyle" data-bind="koGrid: { data: people }"></div>
```

You can see this example in the `cp8-kogrid` branch. Except for needing to manually specify, through style of CSS, the dimensions of the grid itself, everything else is automatic. You get row sorting by clicking on the columns, the ability to toggle columns visibility, a scrollbar for overflow, item counts, and the columns can be reordered by dragging them. The biggest downside is that the data isn't rendered using a real table element, it's rendered using just a bunch of `div` elements.

Of course, this is just the basic mode of operation. KoGrid comes with most of the features you would expect from a fully baked grid widget:

- **Column definitions**: This specifies which row properties are displayed as columns.

- **Grouping**: This allows the user to select a column to pivot the table on, grouping all of the rows by matching values of the selected column.

- **Selected rows**: With this, an observable array can be bound against the selected rows for the table. When the `multiSelect` option is false, this can be used to create a master/detail view with the selected row.

- **Templates**: This provides row and cell templates for the grid.

- **Themes**: This specifies themes on a per-grid basis through binding options.

- **Server-side paging**: This provides callbacks that allow the grid to get data asynchronously from an external source.

 If you want a binding that outputs real table elements, and you don't need all of the bells and whistles offered by KoGrid, check out the knockout-table plugin at `https://github.com/mbest/knockout-table`.

Out of any of these features, templates are probably the most important. While their example page puts the templates in line in the viewmodel code, this is not a recommended practice unless you are loading the string from an external source (such as AJAX or the RequireJS text loader). KoGrid also supports using a script element as a template by referencing its ID, such as Knockout's template system. However, the simplest approach is to use a URL string to refer to an HTML partial file as the template:

```
<div data-bind="koGrid: { data: people,
    canSelectRows: false,
    displaySelectionCheckbox: false,
    columnDefs: [
        { field: 'name', displayName: 'Name', width: '*' },
        { field: 'age', displayName: 'Age', width: '*' },
        { field: '', displayName: ' ',
          cellTemplate: 'app/deleteButtonCell.html',
          width: '**'
    }]}" class="gridStyle"></div>
```

The preceding example shows you several grid options as well as the column definition that specifies which columns to show. Note that the last column does not have a property but has a template that will show you a delete button instead.

It is possible to define these options in the viewmodel and pass only a single object to the KoGrid binding; however, this causes the viewmodel to be tightly coupled to its use by a KoGrid, which is a violation of the MVVM pattern. Defining the grid options in the view keeps the viewmodel agnostic with regards to how it is displayed.

The delete button template will be rendered by KoGrid inside the binding context of the cell:

```
<div data-bind="attr: { 'class': 'kgCellText colt' + $index()}">
    <button class="btn btn-xs btn-danger" data-bind="click: function()
{ $parent.$userViewModel.remove($parent.entity) }">Delete</button>
</div>
```

The complete documentation for cell and row templates will not be covered here, but the preceding template demonstrates several important components.

To control its width and position properly, cells need to include the kgCellText class as well as a 0-indexed class for the column it represents. As the cell will be used inside a column loop, it has access to the special binding context property $index() in order to get this value.

The default value for a click binding in Knockout is the current binding context. Inside the cell template, this will be the cell object and not the item from the data array. The bound item can be accessed using `$parent.entity`. To get access to the viewmodel, the grid is bound against `$parent.$userViewModel`. The `$parent` in both these cases is the binding context for the row; when creating row templates, `$data.entity` and `$userViewModel` can be used to access the same properties.

You can see an example of this custom template in the `cp8-kogrid-template` branch.

The complete documentation for KoGrid can be found on its GitHub Wiki page at https://github.com/Knockout-Contrib/KoGrid/wiki.

# Knockout Bootstrap

Twitter Bootstrap has several beautiful jQuery-dependent widgets that can be used from JavaScript or in some cases, with their `data-*` attributes. If you are using Knockout, though, some work needs to be done in order to get it to work with observables and to initialize it from binding handlers. Knockout Bootstrap is a popular plugin that addresses this. Unfortunately, at the time of writing this, it hasn't been updated to work with Bootstrap 3 and therefore, some of its features do not work. When working with Knockout 3 and Bootstrap 3, the **ToolTip**, **Popover**, and **Alerts** bindings work correctly, but the **Progress Bar** and **Typeahead** bindings do not work.

Like Knockout Kendo, if you have used the Bootstrap widgets, the bindings in Knockout Bootstrap should be immediately familiar. The bindings are named after their widgets and take an object with the same properties the jQuery plugin initializers take. When sensible, the properties can be bound against:

```
//Tooltip
<p>This is a paragraph with a <span data-bind="tooltip: { title:
tooltipText, placement: 'bottom' }"> tooltip span</span> inside.
</p>

//Popover
<button class="btn btn-primary" data-bind="popover: {template:
'popoverTemplate', title: 'Oh Yea'}">
    Launch Simple Popover
</button>
```

```
//Alerts
<div data-bind="foreach: alerts">
    <div data-bind="alert: $data"></div>
</div>
```

These can all be seen in the `cp8-knockout-bootstrap` branch. One thing to note is
that the alert binding does not remove alerts from the bound array when they are
closed on the UI, though it will show or hide array elements as they are added
or removed.

 The complete documentation for Knockout Bootstrap is available at
`http://billpull.com/knockout-bootstrap`.

# Knockout Switch-Case

Despite being a plugin that targets a single, specific use case, Knockout Switch-Case's
popularity on GitHub is evidence that a switch/case control flow binding is a very
useful tool. Instead of writing out a series of `if`/`ifnot` bindings, a single case-switch
binding can be used:

```
<div data-bind="switch: orderStatus">
    <div data-bind="case: 'shipped'">
        Your order has been shipped. Your tracking number is <span
data-bind="text: trackingNumber"></span>.
    </div>
    <div data-bind="case: 'pending'">
        Your order is being processed. Please be patient.
    </div>
    <div data-bind="case: 'incomplete'">
        Your order could not be processed. Please go back and complete
the missing data.
    </div>
    <div data-bind="case: $default">
        Please call customer service to determine the status of your
order.
    </div>
</div>
```

The preceding example can be seen in the `cp8-case-switch` branch.

The switch binding can also act on truthy values. This can be done by looking for the first matching value in a series:

```
<div data-bind="switch: true">
    <div data-bind="case: trackingNumber">
        Your order has been shipped.
    </div>
    <div data-bind="case: isReady">
        Your order is being processed.
    </div>
    <div data-bind="casenot: isComplete">
        Your order has been processed.
    </div>
    <div data-bind="case: $else">
        Your order could not be processed.
    </div>
</div>
```

Or, it can be done by serving as a shorthand for a pair of `if`/`ifnot` bindings:

```
<div data-bind="switch: isReady">
    <div data-bind="case: true">You are ready!</div>
    <div data-bind="case: false">You are not ready!</div>
</div>
```

The switch-case binding can also be used as a container-less binding in any combination of the preceding cases.

As you might have noticed, there are also special `$default` and `$else` options that can be used if no matching value is found.

> The source code for Knockout Switch-Case is available on GitHub at
> `https://github.com/mbest/knockout-switch-case`.

# Knockout Projections

Using a computed observable to filter or project an observable array is an incredibly common operation; I don't think I've ever seen a Knockout project that didn't do this at least once. Knockout Projections is a plugin that adds a map and filter function to observable arrays, which creates a computed observable that only recomputes it's callback on dependent elements that have changed instead of re-evaluating every single dependent element.

Steven Sanderson introduced this plugin via his blog at
http://blog.stevensanderson.com/2013/12/03.

To better understand the problem this plugin solves, we are going to look at the
example Sanderson uses on his blog to illustrate the differences between a normal
computed observable array and an array made with Knockout Projections.

Consider the following model:

```
function Product(data) {
    this.name = ko.observable(data.name);
    this.isSelected = ko.observable(false);
}
function PageViewModel() {
    // Some data, perhaps loaded via an Ajax call
    this.products = ko.observableArray([ /* several Products /* ]);
    this.selectedProducts = ko.computed(function() {
        return this.products().filter(function(product) {
            return product.isSelected();
        });
    }, this);
}
```

This `selectedProducts` computed is defined using the standard ES5 Array's `filter`
function, calling `products()` returns the underlying JavaScript array. Every time it
runs, it will loop over all of the products and return an array of every element with
`isSelected() === true`. The problem here is that computed observables always
rerun when any of their dependencies change; the computed can only perform
re-evaluation by running its callback, and has to recheck every single product
every time it runs. This does not scale very well; it runs in O(N) time.

When using Knockout Projections, you will create this same computed using the
`filter` function on the observable array itself:

```
this.selectedProducts = this.products.filter(function(product) {
    return product.isSelected();
});
```

This creates a read-only observable array that creates individual dependencies on
each product's `isSelected` observable. When a product is changed, the callback is
run against only that product, and the `selectedProducts` array is updated with the
change. Performance now has a fixed cost: no matter how large the array gets, the
callback will only be run once per dependency change. The declaring code is also
shorter and easier to read!

Knockout Projections also creates a map function on observables, which runs a callback that produces an array transformation instead of a filter. For example, you can create an observable array of product names that only received updates when individual names were changed:

```
this.productNames = this.products.map(function(product) {
    return product.name();
});
```

As the read-only arrays created by filter and map are also observable arrays, these methods can be chained together:

```
this.selectedNames = this.selectedProducts.map(function(product) {
    return product.name();
});
```

The performance gain from using Knockout Projections is minor in small arrays but significant in larger ones. If you are working with even medium-sized data sets, using Knockout Projections is a no-brainer.

# Knockout-ES5

Knockout-ES5 is a plugin for Knockout that uses JavaScript getters and setters to hide observables behind object properties, allowing your application code to use standard syntax to work with them. Basically, it gets rid of the observable parentheses:

Take a look at the following code:

```
var latestOrder = this.orders()[this.orders().length - 1];
latestOrder.isShipped(true);
```

The preceding code becomes this:

```
var latestOrder = this.orders[this.orders.length - 1];
latestOrder.isShipped = true;
```

If you remember the Durandal observable plugin, it's very similar; they even came out around the same time. The biggest difference between the two is that Durandal's observable plugin performs deep object conversion, and Knockout ES5 performs shallow conversion.

To convert a viewmodel's properties to observables, call `ko.track`:

```
function Person(init) {
    var self = this,
        data = init || {};

    self.name = data.name || '';
    self.age = data.age || '';
    self.alive = data.alive !== undefined ? data.alive : true;
    self.job = data.job || '';

    ko.track(self);
}
```

To optionally specify which properties are to be converted in order to pass an array of names, take a look at the following code:

```
ko.track(self, ['name', 'age']);
```

Observables that already exist on the model, such as those created with `ko.observable` or `ko.computed`, are also converted into ES5 properties by `ko.track`. Optionally, you can define computed observables using `ko.defineProperty`:

```
ko.defineProperty(self, 'canRemove', function() {
    return !self.alive;
});
```

The third parameter follows the same rules as the first parameter sent to `ko.computed`; a function will be used to create a read-only computed, or an object can be used to supply a read/write function.

Once observables have been created, you can access them with `ko.getObservable`:

```
ko.getObservable(self, 'age').subscribe(function(newValue) {
    console.log(self.name + ' age was changed to ' + newValue);
});
```

This is useful while applying extenders or adding subscriptions. Extenders can also be applied by creating observables with `ko.observable` before calling `ko.track`.

An example of all of these techniques can be seen in the `cp8-es5` branch.

# Browser support

As Knockout-ES5 uses JavaScript getters and setters, it will not work in browsers that do not support this feature. This is not a feature that can be shimmed or polyfilled with scripts.

Knockout gets a lot of flak for the syntax that results from the decision to make observable object functions. Going by the popularity of questions on Stack Overflow, it is certainly one of the most confusing aspects to newcomers. The decision to do this was made so that support for older browsers such as Internet Explorer 6, which doesn't support JavaScript getters and setters, was possible. Now that Internet Explorer 6 is finally starting to lose its death grip on the browser market share, this supportability issue is becoming less and less important to web developers. Unfortunately, Internet Explorer didn't add support for ES5 getters and setters until IE 9, which is still a high bar for most projects.

Realistically, as using Knockout ES5 has such a drastic impact on application syntax, switching to it on a that is project already underway is rarely feasible. Knockout ES5 should only be considered for new projects that do not have an old browser support requirement.

# Summary

Narrowing down the plugins and libraries to include in this chapter was difficult. Knockout's Wiki page on GitHub contains a long list of plugins (`https://github.com/knockout/knockout/wiki/Plugins`)—far too many to discuss here. If you are working with Knockout, you are encouraged to check out the community offerings, as it could end up saving you a lot of work. Not all of these plugins will be useful to everyone or every project, but hopefully, they give you an idea of what can be done with Knockout and motivate you to share some of your own work with the community.

In the next chapter, we will be taking a deep dive into Knockout's internals to see how it works.

# 9
# Under the Hood

We have covered the Knockout basics, learned how to extend Knockout's binding system, and seen how to organize applications. Now, it's time to indulge our inner tinkerers. In this chapter, we will look at the internals of Knockout to see what makes it tick. By the end of this chapter, you should be familiar with how Knockout handles the following:

- Dependency tracking
- The prototype chain
- Parsing binding attribute expressions
- Applying bindings
- Templating

In addition to this, we will also look at the `ko.utils` namespace, which provides lots of useful tools for common actions.

 Note that all of the code discussed in this chapter is based on the Knockout 3.2 release. It is possible, and likely, that parts of this will change in the future.

# Dependency tracking

Binding handlers and computed observables need to re-evaluate when their observable dependencies update. This means keeping track of dependencies and subscribing to them. Three objects make up the dependency-tracking feature: observables, computed observables, and the dependency-detection module.

Here's the basic overview. When a computed is evaluated, it asks `ko.dependencyDetection` to start tracking things. When observables are accessed, they register themselves with `ko.dependencyDetection`. When the computed is done evaluating, it records all of the registered dependencies and subscribes to each of them.

Okay, now let's look at some code.

# ko.dependencyDetection

The dependency detection module is very small—small enough to reproduce here in its entirety, actually:

```
ko.computedContext = ko.dependencyDetection = (function () {
  var outerFrames = [],
  currentFrame,
  lastId = 0;

  function getId() {
    return ++lastId;
  }

  function begin(options) {
    outerFrames.push(currentFrame);
    currentFrame = options;
  }

  function end() {
    currentFrame = outerFrames.pop();
  }

  return {
    begin: begin,
    end: end,
    registerDependency: function (subscribable) {
      if (currentFrame) {
        if (!ko.isSubscribable(subscribable))
        throw new Error("Only subscribable things can act as
          dependencies");
        currentFrame.callback(subscribable, subscribable._id ||
          (subscribable._id = getId()));
      }
    },
```

```
      ignore: function (callback, callbackTarget, callbackArgs) {
        try {
          begin();
          return callback.apply(callbackTarget, callbackArgs || []);
        } finally {
          end();
        }
      },
      getDependenciesCount: function () {
        if (currentFrame)
        return currentFrame.computed.getDependenciesCount();
      },
      isInitial: function() {
        if (currentFrame)
        return currentFrame.isInitial;
      }
    };
})();
```

The preceding code is using the revealing module pattern to hide the internal variables for outerFrames, currentFrame, lastId, and the getId function.

> For more information on the revealing module pattern, check out Todd Motto's blog at http://toddmotto.com/mastering-the-module-pattern.

The idea here is that begin is called with either a frame that can be used for tracking, or it is called with nothing to disable tracking. When end is called, the previous frame is popped off and set to the current frame. A **frame** is a layer that tracks dependencies; a frame exists inside of another frame, but only the current frame will register dependencies when they are accessed. This allows dependency tracking to occur recursively, while each layer receives only its immediate dependencies.

The options object that is passed to begin should expose the following properties:

- callback: This is a function that receives a dependency and its ID when a dependency registers itself

- computed: This is the computed observable that performs the dependency tracking on the frame

- isInitial: This is a Boolean that indicates whether this is the first time dependency tracking has been requested for the current frame

When `registerDependency` is called, the current frame's callback is passed to the dependency and its ID. The ID is a sequentially generated number, which is assigned to the dependency if it is missing.

The `ignore` function provides an easy wrapper around `begin` and `end` inside a `try/finally` block. The call to `begin` has no options, so it will not trigger dependency detection. This makes it easy to evaluate data in situations where you know dependency detection will not, or should not, be used. Knockout does this inside several binding handlers as well as inside the `notifySubscribers` function of subscribables.

The last two properties, which are `getDependenciesCount` and `isInitial`, expose the properties of the same name on the current frame.

# Registering dependencies

When an observable is read, it has to notify `ko.dependencyDetection` in order to indicate that a dependency has been accessed. Because computeds and observables are both descendants of subscribables, which do not register dependencies, each of them has their own similar dependency registration logic.

The observable implementation happens when the observable is called with no arguments:

```
function observable() {
  if (arguments.length > 0) {
    /* write new value */
  }
  else {
    // Read
    ko.dependencyDetection.registerDependency(observable);
    return _latestValue;
  }
}
```

After registering itself as a dependency, it returns its current value. The computed version is almost identical:

```
function dependentObservable() {
  if (arguments.length > 0) {
    /* write new value */
  } else {
    ko.dependencyDetection.registerDependency
      (dependentObservable);
```

```
        if (_needsEvaluation) //suppressChangeNotification
        evaluateImmediate(true);
        return _latestValue;
    }
}
```

The only difference here is that because computeds can be evaluated asynchronously, the `read` function checks whether a re-evaluation is needed before returning its value.

There isn't much else to say regarding this. The observable array type makes no changes to the registration process. In fact, it couldn't make any changes. Dependency registration is an internal logic for observables; it can't be overridden.

# Subscribing to dependencies

The prototype for all observables is the subscribable. The subscribable prototype provides two functions for dependency work: `subscribe` and `notifySubscribers`.

The `subscribe` function creates a subscription on the subscribable. The subscription doesn't do anything on its own, it's just an object with a `callback` and `dispose` property (it has other properties; these are just the relevant ones). The subscription is stored in the `_subscriptions` object and the internal-use property. As subscriptions can be attached to named events, the subscriptions object has an array for each event:

```
_subscriptions: {
  change: [sub1, sub2],
  beforeChange: [sub3, sub4]
};
```

When a subscription is created without a name, it is attached to the change event by default. The other standard event is the `beforeChange` event, which is fired by observables just before they update. This is the write logic from the observable:

```
function observable() {
  if (arguments.length > 0) {
    // Ignore writes if the value hasn't changed
    if (observable.isDifferent(_latestValue, arguments[0])) {
      observable.valueWillMutate();
      _latestValue = arguments[0];
      observable.valueHasMutated();
    }
    return this; // Permits chained assignments
  }
  else {
    // Read code
```

```
    }
  }
//...
observable.valueHasMutated = function () {
  observable["notifySubscribers"](_latestValue);
}
observable.valueWillMutate = function () {
  observable["notifySubscribers"](_latestValue, "beforeChange");
}
```

Before an observable is updated, it calls valueWillMutate, and afterwards, it calls valueHasMutated. Both of these are wrappers around the notifySubscribers function, with the first providing the beforeChange event name:

```
notifySubscribers: function (valueToNotify, event) {
  event = event || defaultEvent;
  if (this.hasSubscriptionsForEvent(event)) {
    try {
      // Begin suppressing dependency detection
      ko.dependencyDetection.begin();
      for (var a = this._subscriptions[event].slice(0),
      i = 0, subscription;
      subscription = a[i]; ++i) {
        if (!subscription.isDisposed)
        subscription.callback(valueToNotify);
      }
    } finally {
      // End suppressing dependency detection
      ko.dependencyDetection.end();
    }
  }
}
```

Once again, the event name is optional and defaults to change when omitted. It also checks to make sure subscriptions for the event exist before it starts. Then, it disables dependency detection. If it didn't disable dependency detection, then a false dependency would be established between the original writer of the new value and subscribers of the current observable.

> This basic publish/subscribe implementation can easily be used to create a messaging system. In fact, Ryan Niemeyer has created a plugin to do just that (see https://github.com/rniemeyer/knockout-postbox).

The primary work is to loop through the subscriptions and pass the current value to the subscriptions callback. A check is performed to ensure that the subscription didn't get disposed, as it is possible that one subscription is disposed because of another. Finally, the previous block of code ends the current frame of dependency detection.

With these three pieces, Knockout provides a simple and performant dependency tracking system.

# Subscribing to observable arrays

Prototypically speaking, observable arrays are still observables, but because their changes are primarily their contents and not their values, they have a lot of additional logic that ensures performant notifications.

## Standard array functions

JavaScript has had a standard set of array functions since ECMAScript's first edition, so you should already be familiar with them. The headache they cause for Knockout is that they modify the contents of the array directly. Since array subscribers expect to be notified to changes in the array's content, Knockout provides their own implementation for `observableArray`. This implementation makes calls to the standard notification functions on observables before calling the original array function. The `slice` function is skipped, since it is a read-only function and doesn't needs to notify subscribers:

```
ko.utils.arrayForEach(["pop", "push", "reverse", "shift", "sort",
  "splice", "unshift"], function (methodName) {
  ko.observableArray['fn'][methodName] = function () {
    var underlyingArray = this.peek();
    this.valueWillMutate();
    this.cacheDiffForKnownOperation(underlyingArray, methodName,
      arguments);
    var methodCallResult = underlyingArray[methodName].apply(
      underlyingArray, arguments);
    this.valueHasMutated();
    return methodCallResult;
  };
});
```

This function has barely changed since Knockout 1.0, where it added the methods to each instance instead of the observable array's `fn` prototype. The only addition is the call to `cacheDiffForKnownOperation`, which works with the internal `trackArrayChanges` extender to provide smaller, faster change notifications for incremental updates to the array. Prior to this extender, observable arrays broadcasted their entire contents on every update.

This function is not too different from the `write` function of normal observables; it calls `valueWillMutate` before performing an update, and it calls `valueHasMutated` afterward. Instead of setting its own value, it just applies the original method name to the underlying array.

The `slice` function is even simpler. It does not cause subscriptions to fire, as it is read-only. All it does is wrap the original function on the underlying array:

```
ko.utils.arrayForEach(["slice"], function (methodName) {
  ko.observableArray['fn'][methodName] = function () {
    var underlyingArray = this();
    return underlyingArray[methodName].apply(underlyingArray,
      arguments);
  };
});
```

## The utility methods

In addition to the standard methods, Knockout also provides friendly functions to common array changes that JavaScript, for some reason, still hasn't bothered to implement: `remove`, `removeAll`, `destroy`, `destroyAll`, and `replace`.

You should be able to guess what these functions look like by now; peek to get the underlying array, call `valueWillMutate`, make some changes, and then finish with `valueHasMutated`. The interesting part about the preceding functions is the arguments they take. If you pass an object to `remove`, it will predictably remove that object from the array if it exists. However, if you pass a function, it will be used as a predicate, removing any elements in the array, which causes the predicate to return truthy (I'm very fond of this pattern):

```
remove: function (valueOrPredicate) {
  var underlyingArray = this.peek();
  var removedValues = [];
  var predicate = typeof valueOrPredicate == "function" &&
    !ko.isObservable(valueOrPredicate) ? valueOrPredicate :
    function (value) { return value === valueOrPredicate; };
  for (var i = 0; i < underlyingArray.length; i++) {
    var value = underlyingArray[i];
    if (predicate(value)) {
      //Remove element, add to removedValues
    }
  }
  if (removedValues.length) {
```

```
        this.valueHasMutated();
    }
    return removedValues;
}
```

This works by converting single values into a predicate that checks for strict equality. The check for `!ko.isObservable(valueOrPredicate)` is important as observables are functions but should be treated as values here and not as predicates.

This same pattern is used for `destroy`, except that it marks the observables with the `_destory` property instead of removing them.

The `removeAll` and `destroyAll` functions are also overloaded: they can take an array of values to be removed, or it can remove all elements if no argument is provided. In the case where an array of values is provided, they just call `remove`/`destroy` with a predicate based on the array:

```
removeAll: function (arrayOfValues) {
    // If you passed zero args, we remove everything
    if (arrayOfValues === undefined) {
        //remove all elements
    }
    return this['remove'](function (value) {
        return ko.utils.arrayIndexOf(arrayOfValues, value) >= 0;
    });
}
```

# The prototype chain

Back in *Chapter 1*, *Knockout Essentials*, I showed you this diagram:

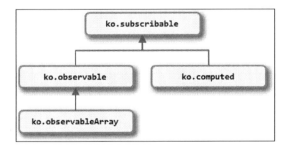

The way functions are inherited by these objects is not through the normal JavaScript prototype chain, where a constructor function has its prototype assigned to an object. This is because observables are functions and not objects, and functions cannot be created with constructors or the Object.create function. Standard JavaScript prototypical inheritance doesn't work for functions. To see how Knockout shares methods, let's look at how subscribable and its descendant observable are constructed.

First, the base methods for subscribables are defined on the fn object:

```
var ko_subscribable_fn = {
  subscribe: function (callback, target, event) { /* logic */ },
  notifySubscribers: function (value, event) { /* logic */ },
  limit: function(limitFunction) { /* logic */ },
  hasSubscriptionsForEvent: function(event) { /* logic */ },
  getSubscriptionsCount: function () { /* logic */ },
  isDifferent: function(oldValue, newValue) { /* logic */ },
  extend: applyExtenders
};
ko.subscribable['fn'] = ko_subscribable_fn;
```

This is added to subscribables during the construction:

```
ko.subscribable = function () {
  ko.utils.setPrototypeOfOrExtend(this, ko.subscribable['fn']);
  this._subscriptions = {};
}
```

The setPrototypeOfOrExtend method will either assign the __proto__ property of an object—something higher IE versions can't do—or use ko.utils.extend to extend the object.

Observables are built differently. Their *factory* method returns an internally built object, which uses both ko.subscribable.call and setPrototypeOfOrExtend to inherit methods:

```
ko.observable = function (initialValue) {
  var _latestValue = initialValue;

  function observable() {
    //build observable
  }
  ko.subscribable.call(observable);
  ko.utils.setPrototypeOfOrExtend(observable, ko.observable
    ['fn']);
```

```
observable.peek = function() { return _latestValue };
observable.valueHasMutated = function () {
  observable["notifySubscribers"](_latestValue);
}
observable.valueWillMutate = function () {
  observable["notifySubscribers"](_latestValue, "beforeChange");
}

return observable;
}
```

An observable is built and then run through the subscribable's constructor, extended with the `observable[''fn'']` object, and finally has its own methods added.

# The ko.isObservable function

In standard JavaScript inheritance, the `instanceof` operator can be used to check whether an object, or any of its prototypes, has a constructor that matches the supplied function. Because Knockout isn't using standard inheritance, it cannot use the `instanceof` operator; instead Knockout uses the following code for the `ko.isObservable` function.

```
var protoProperty = ko.observable.protoProperty = "__ko_proto__";
ko.observable['fn'][protoProperty] = ko.observable;

ko.hasPrototype = function(instance, prototype) {
  if ((instance === null) || (instance === undefined) ||
    (instance[protoProperty] === undefined)) return false;
  if (instance[protoProperty] === prototype) return true;
  return ko.hasPrototype(instance[protoProperty], prototype); //
    Walk the prototype chain
};

ko.isObservable = function (instance) {
  return ko.hasPrototype(instance, ko.observable);
}
```

Knockout defines a __ko_proto__ property on the `observable[''fn'']` object, which is set to the `ko.observable` object. This custom prototype property is used by `hasPrototype` in place of the `instanceof` operator to determine whether an instanced object is an observable.

# The binding expression parser

The expressions written in data-bind attributes are not truly JavaScript or JSON, though they look very similar. Knockout has its own parser to convert these attributes into JavaScript. Say you write a data-bind attribute like this one:

```
data-bind="value: name, visible: showName"
```

Then, the binding provider's job is to return an object like this:

```
{
  value: function() { return name; },
  visible: function() { return showName; }
}
```

The default binding provider does this using the `ko.expressionRewriting` module, which is responsible for calling binding preprocessors and returning a JSON-esque string. Internally, this is done using regex to parse the full attribute into a key/value pair array. This might sound messy, but it gets the job done. That being said, even for an *under the hood* look, the details are not very relevant to Knockout, as the parsing is general purpose. If you are still curious, the code is located at `https://github.com/knockout/knockout/blob/master/src/binding/expressionRewriting.js`, and its inline comments are better than average.

After parsing the data-bind attribute, the array of key/value pairs is iterated to build an array of JSON-esque strings:

```
function processKeyValue(key, val) {
  var writableVal;
  function callPreprocessHook(obj) {
    return (obj && obj['preprocess']) ? (val =
      obj['preprocess'](val, key, processKeyValue)) : true;
  }
  if (!bindingParams) {
    if (!callPreprocessHook(ko['getBindingHandler'](key)))
    return;

    if (twoWayBindings[key] && (writableVal =
      getWriteableValue(val))) {
      //provide a write method in case the value
      // isn't a writable observable.
      propertyAccessorResultStrings.push("'" + key +
        "':function(_z){" + writableVal + "=_z}");
    }
  }
}
```

```
if (makeValueAccessors) {
  val = 'function(){return ' + val + ' }';
}
resultStrings.push("'" + key + "':" + val);
}
```

The key is used to look up the binding handler to call its `preprocess` function. If it returns falsy, the processing stops, as the binding was removed. The `makeValueAccessors` property will be true when it comes from `getBindingAccessors` and false when it comes from `getBindings`. The result is then added to a running list.

The `twoWayBindings` block adds a special function string to `propertyAccessorResultStrings`, which is checked after all the other bindings keys are finished:

```
if (propertyAccessorResultStrings.length)
  processKeyValue('_ko_property_writers', "{" +
    propertyAccessorResultStrings.join(",") + " }");
```

This adds one extra binding property, `_ko_property_writers`, which is a function that will return a binding object that can be used to write to bound properties instead of reading from them. We will come back to this in just a minute.

Finally, the running list of strings is returned with a join:

```
return resultStrings.join(",");
```

The resulting string from the example binding will look like this:

```
'value': function() { return name; }, 'visible': function() {
  return showName; '_ko_property_writers':function(){return
  {'value':function(_z){ name =_z} } } }
```

The binding provider turns this string into a real object by putting the string inside a function body and calling the function with the binding context and the element being bound:

```
var rewrittenBindings = ko.expressionRewriting.
  preProcessBindings(bindingsString, options),
  functionBody = "with($context){with($data||{}){return{" +
    rewrittenBindings + "}}}";
  return new Function("$context", "$element", functionBody);
```

This use of new Function causes Knockout's default binding provider to fail in environments using a **Content Security Policy (CSP)** that blocks new Function and eval, such as in Google Chrome Extensions. Knockout Secure Binding, which is a binding provider that does not use new Function, allows Knockout to be used with a CSP (see https://github.com/brianmhunt/knockout-secure-binding).

When this function is evaluated with the binding context and element, it produces the final binding object:

```
{
  value: function() { return name; },
  visible: function() { return showName; },
  _ko_property_writers: function (){
    return {'value':function(_z){query=_z} }
  }
}
```

# Knockout property writers

We haven't covered the _ko_property_writers property yet, because it's surprising to most people and would have been distracting. The role of this property is to expose writing functions for nonobservable values so that two-way binding handlers can still update their values. They aren't observable, so notifications won't occur, but it's still a supported scenario.

This special binding is carried on the binding accessor. When two-way bindings, such as value, need to update the viewmodel they, call ko.expressionRewriting. writeValueToProperty:

```
writeValueToProperty: function(property, allBindings, key, value,
checkIfDifferent) {
  if (!property || !ko.isObservable(property)) {
    var propWriters = allBindings.get('_ko_property_writers');
    if (propWriters && propWriters[key])
    propWriters[key](value);
  } else if (ko.isWriteableObservable(property) &&
    (!checkIfDifferent || property.peek() !== value)) {
    property(value);
  }
}
```

This is an undocumented part of the API, so it is subject to changing without notice.

If the property is not observable and a property writer exists for it, then it is used to update the value. If the property is observable, the property is written directly.

# Applying bindings

The binding application process takes place primarily in the `bindingAttributeSyntax` module, which defines the `ko.bindingContext` class as well as the `ko.applyBindings` method. The high-level overview looks like this:

1. The `ko.applyBindings` method is called with the viewmodel.
2. A binding context is constructed using the viewmodel.
3. The binding provider is retrieved from `ko.bindingProvider.instance`.
4. Knockout works with the DOM tree:
   - It is passed through the binding provider's node preprocessor (except the root node)
   - The binding handlers for the node are constructed using the binding provider
   - The binding handlers are sorted by ensuring that any bindings in their `after` property are loaded first
   - The binding handlers are iterated through, calling each handler's `init` and `update` function.

The first three steps are pretty straightforward; even the walking algorithm is just a simple recursion that applies bindings to a node and then iterates over its children to preprocess and bind them. The real meat of this process is the `applyBindingsToNodeInternal` function, which actually does the work of applying bindings to a node.

The first half of the function is safety checks. We are going to skip the code for this, as it's not very important to understanding how the binding part works. As we have already covered how the binding provider generates bindings, we are only going to look at the last two bullet points.

# Sorting binding handlers

Knockout uses a topological sort to order the binding handlers.

If you are unfamiliar with topological sorting, remember that it comes from graph theory. We will not go into the details of graph theory here (if you are interested, Google can tell you all about it), but a topological sort is basically an ordering of elements, which ensures that all dependencies of an element come before the element itself. Topological sorts do not guarantee the same order every time; it's just that no dependency cycles exist.

This is the sort function that Knockout uses to order binding handlers; it is a fairly common implementation:

```
function topologicalSortBindings(bindings) {
  // Depth-first sort
  var result = [],                    // The list of key/handler pairs
    that we will return
  bindingsConsidered = {},    // A temporary record of which
    bindings are already in 'result'
  cyclicDependencyStack = []; // Keeps track of a depth-search so
    that, if there's a cycle, we know which bindings caused it
  ko.utils.objectForEach(bindings, function pushBinding
    (bindingKey) {
    if (!bindingsConsidered[bindingKey]) {
      var binding = ko['getBindingHandler'](bindingKey);
      if (binding) {
        // First add dependencies (if any) of the current binding
        if (binding['after']) {
          cyclicDependencyStack.push(bindingKey);
          ko.utils.arrayForEach(binding['after'],
            function(bindingDependencyKey) {
            if (bindings[bindingDependencyKey]) {
              if (ko.utils.arrayIndexOf(cyclicDependencyStack,
                bindingDependencyKey) !== -1) {
                throw Error("Cannot combine the following
                  bindings, because they have a cyclic dependency:
                  " + cyclicDependencyStack.join(", "));
              } else {
                pushBinding(bindingDependencyKey);
              }
            }
          });
          cyclicDependencyStack.length--;
        }
```

```
        // Next add the current binding
        result.push({ key: bindingKey, handler: binding });
    }
    bindingsConsidered[bindingKey] = true;
    }
});

    return result;
}
```

This function loops through the supplied bindings, skipping bindings it has already processed; if it has an `after` property, it starts the dependency check. It pushes the current binding into the array-tracking dependencies, and then loops through each of the bindings in the `after` property. If a dependent binding is already found to be in the array of dependencies Knockout throws an exception, it would mean a cycling dependency. If the dependent binding is not found, it recurses into the loop handler so that its dependencies are checked.

After the dependent bindings are checked, the last element in the array of dependencies is removed and the current binding is pushed to the array of results and the array of already processed bindings. If a future binding requires it as a dependency, the loop handler will return immediately, indicating that the future binding is safe to continue.

# Running the binding handlers

After getting the binding handlers in the proper order, they are iterated through. One last safety check is made in order to ensure that if the node is a comment node, the binding handler is allowed for virtual elements. Then the `init` and `update` functions are called inside a `try`/`catch` block:

```
// Run init, ignoring any dependencies
var handlerInitFn = bindingKeyAndHandler.handler["init"];
if (typeof handlerInitFn == "function") {
  ko.dependencyDetection.ignore(function() {
    var initResult = handlerInitFn(node,
    getValueAccessor(bindingKey),
    allBindings,
    bindingContext['$data'],
    bindingContext);

    // If this binding handler claims to control descendant
      bindings, make a note of this
```

```
    if (initResult && initResult['controlsDescendantBindings']) {
        if (bindingHandlerThatControlsDescendantBindings !==
          undefined)
        throw new Error("Multiple bindings (" +
          bindingHandlerThatControlsDescendantBindings + " and " +
          bindingKey + ") are trying to control descendant bindings
          of the same element. You cannot use these bindings
          together on the same element.");
        bindingHandlerThatControlsDescendantBindings = bindingKey;
    }
  });
}
```

The whole thing is run in a scope with dependency detection disabled, as the init function does not run twice. The init handler passes all the required arguments, and the result is checked to see whether this handler wants to control descendant bindings. If it isn't the first handler to control descendant bindings, then Knockout throws an exception:

```
// Run update in its own computed wrapper
var handlerUpdateFn = bindingKeyAndHandler.handler["update"];
if (typeof handlerUpdateFn == "function") {
  ko.dependentObservable(
    function() {
      handlerUpdateFn(node,
      getValueAccessor(bindingKey),
      allBindings,
      bindingContext['$data'],
      bindingContext);
    },
    null,
    { disposeWhenNodeIsRemoved: node }
  );
}
```

The update handler is run inside of a computed observable (dependantObservable was the original name for computeds and is still used in the source code), which will automatically rerun it when dependencies change. This is one of my favorite parts of Knockout: binding handlers rerun automatically when observable dependencies change because *they are inside observables themselves.*

Once the binding handlers have all been looped through, `applyBindingsToNodeInternal` returns with an object that tells its caller whether or not to recurse into the current node's children using the flag from the `init` handler's result:

```
return {
  'shouldBindDescendants': bindingHandlerThatControls
    DescendantBindings === undefined
};
```

# Templates

Knockout's template system is incredibly flexible: it works with *anonymous* templates, named templates, and allows the engine that renders templates to be overridden. The template binding is also used by the `foreach` binding, which is just a syntactic sugar for the `{ foreach: someExpression }` template. To understand how the template system works, let's start with the template-binding handler.

# The template binding handler

The `init` function of the template binding understands that templates can either be named (loaded from a source) or inline (loaded using the contents of the bound element):

```
'init': function(element, valueAccessor) {
  // Support anonymous templates
  var bindingValue = ko.utils.unwrapObservable(valueAccessor());
  if (typeof bindingValue == "string" || bindingValue['name']) {
    // It's a named template - clear the element
    ko.virtualElements.emptyNode(element);
  } else {
    var templateNodes = ko.virtualElements.childNodes(element),
    container = ko.utils.moveCleanedNodesToContainer
      Element(templateNodes);
    new ko.templateSources.anonymousTemplate
      (element)['nodes'](container);
  }
  return { 'controlsDescendantBindings': true };
}
```

If the binding value is just a string, or if the binding value is an object with a `name` property, then we are using a named source and the only work that needs to be done is to empty the node. Named sources need to be changed when the name of the template changes, so all of the work of actually rendering the template is in the `update` method.

If it's an anonymous template, `moveCleanedNodesToContainerElement` removes the children from the element and places them in a `div` container, but the `div` container isn't placed in the DOM. A new anonymous template source is created with the element, and the `div` container is passed to the template's `nodes` function. The `nodes` function stores the container with `utils.domData`.

A **template source** is an object that is used by the template engine to provide the DOM that is required to render the template. It must provide either a `nodes` function that returns a container with the nodes to be used, or a `text` function that provides a stringified version of the same. The `ko.templateSources` array contains two template source types: `domElement` for named sources and `anonymousTemplate` for inline sources.

Finally, the `init` function returns `{ 'controlsDescendantBindings': true }`.

The `update` function has three different branches: branches that render a single template, branches that render an array of templates with `foreach`, and branches that remove everything if an `if` (or `ifnot`) binding is present and false. The last branch doesn't need much explanation, and the first two branches are very functionally similar: they call `renderTemplate` on the template engine, which returns an array of DOM nodes that are then added to the DOM. After this, they each call `applyBindings` on the template.

# The template engine

The template engine is responsible for generating DOM nodes. It can't be used on its own though, as it's just a base class. When `renderTemplate` is called on the base template engine, it calls `makeTemplateSource` and passes the result to `renderTemplateSource`.

The default `makeTemplateSource` method takes a template parameter. If a template is a string, it will try to find a script by that name and create a `domElement` source. If the template is a node, it will create and return a new `anonymousTemplate` source from it.

The default `renderTemplateSource` method is not implemented and will throw an error. A template implementation must override this method in order to work.

Knockout provides two template engine implementations out of the box: native and jQuery.tmpl. The jQuery.tmpl engine hasn't been under development since 2011, and I think Knockout's continued inclusion with the standard distribution is probably more backwards-compatibility than anyone really needs. It's there, but we are going to ignore it.

The native template engine overrides `renderTemplateSource` with this:

```
function (templateSource, bindingContext, options) {
  // IE<9 cloneNode doesn't work properly
  var useNodesIfAvailable = !(ko.utils.ieVersion < 9),
    templateNodesFunc = useNodesIfAvailable ?
      templateSource['nodes'] : null,
    templateNodes = templateNodesFunc ? templateSource['nodes']() :
      null;

  if (templateNodes) {
    return ko.utils.makeArray(templateNodes.cloneNode
      (true).childNodes);
  } else {
    var templateText = templateSource['text']();
    return ko.utils.parseHtmlFragment(templateText);
  }
};
```

If `nodes` is present, it will be used to get the template node container, clone it, and return it. If it's in an higher IE, where clone doesn't work, or if `nodes` isn't provided, the text source will be parsed by `ko.utils` and will be returned.

The template engine does not add the nodes to the DOM and does not bind them; it just returns them. The template binding takes care of this part after it gets the generated template from the template engine.

# The ko.utils reference

The `ko.utils` namespace is Knockout's bucket for utility functions. Not all of these functions are publicly exposed—at least not in a usable way. Knockout's minification process obfuscates more than half of them. As the unobfuscated methods are a public API that Knockout has committed to providing, changing them would be a major change. Despite considering all of the exposed methods on the `ko.utils` part of the API, Knockout does not provide any documentation for them.

Here is a complete list of the public functions on `ko.utils` as of Knockout 3.2:

- `addOrRemoveItem(array, item, included)`: If `included` is `true`, it will add the item to the array if it is not already there; if `included` is `false`, it will remove the item from the array if it is present.

- `arrayFilter(array, predicate)`: This returns an array of elements from the array that returns `true` from the predicate using `predicate(element, index)`.

- `arrayFirst(array, predicate, predicateOwner)`: This returns the first element in the array that returns `true` from the predicate using `predicate.call(predicateOwner, element, index)`. This makes `predicateOwner` an optional parameter, which controls this in the predicate.

- `arrayForEach(array, action)`: This calls the action on each element in the array with `action(element, index)`.

- `arrayGetDistinctValues(array)`: This returns an array with only distinct elements from the original array. It uses `ko.utils.arrayIndexOf` to determine the uniqueness.

- `arrayIndexOf(array, item)`: If `Array.prototype.indexOf` is present, `arrayIndexOf(array, item)` will call it, otherwise it will loop the array manually and return the index or `-1` if the element isn't found. This is a polyfill for versions of Internet Explorer less than 9.

- `arrayMap(array, mapping)`: This is not quite a polyfill for `Array.prototype.map`; this function returns an array by calling `mapping(element, index)` on each element of the original array.

- `arrayPushAll(array, valuesToPush)`: This pushes the `valuesToPush` parameter into the `array` parameter. This function handles cases where `valuesToPush` is like an array but is not a real array, such as `HTMLCollection`, where calling `array.push.apply(array, valuesToPush)` would normally fail.

- `arrayRemoveItem(array, itemToRemove)`: This removes the item from the array by either splicing or shifting, depending on the item's index.

- `domData`: This object provides a `get`, `set`, and `clear` method in order to work with arbitrary key/value pairs on DOM nodes. Knockout uses it internally to track the binding information, but it can be used to store anything.

- `domNodeDisposal`: This object provides the following utilities that are related to DOM's cleanup tasks:
  - `addDisposeCallback(node, callback)`: This adds a callback to the node with `domData`. The callback will be used if Knockout removes the node via templating or control flow.
  - `cleanNode(node)`: This runs all the associated disposal callbacks that were registered with `addDisposeCallback`. This function is aliased as `ko.cleanNode`.
  - `cleanExternalData(node)`: This uses jQuery's `cleanData` function to remove data added by jQuery plugins. It does nothing if jQuery is not found.
  - `removeDisposeCallback(node, callback)`: This removes the callback from the node's `domData` function.
  - `removeNode(node)`: This cleans the node with `cleanNode` and then removes it from the DOM. This function is aliased as `ko.removeNode`.

- `Extend(target, source)`: This is a run-of-the-mill extend method; it adds or overwrites all properties on the target with those on the source. It filters source properties with `hasOwnProperty`.

- `fieldsIncludedWithJsonPost`: This is an array of default fields that are used for `postJson` if an `includeFields` option is not specified.

- `getFormFields(form, fieldName)`: This returns all the `input` or `textarea` fields from a form that matches `fieldname`, which can be either a string, a regex, or an object with a test predicate that takes the field's name.

- `objectForEach(obj, action)`: This calls `action(properyName, propetyValue)` on each property in `obj`, filtering it with `hasOwnProperty`.

- `parseHtmlFragment(html)`: If jQuery is present, this function uses its `parseHTML` function; otherwise, it uses a simple internal HTML parse. It returns DOM nodes.

- `parseJson(jsonString)`: This will return a JavaScript object by parsing the supplied string. If the JSON object exists, it will be used; otherwise, `new Function` will be used.

- `peekObservable(value)`: Just like `ko.unwrap`, this is a safety method. If the value is observable, it will return the result of its peek; otherwise, it will just return the value.

- `postJson(urlOrForm, data, options)`: This will perform a post by creating a new form, appending it to the DOM, and calling `submit` on it. The form will use `data` to create its fields. If `urlOrForm` is a form, its fields will be included in the data if they match `options['']includeFields'']` (or `fieldsIncludedWithJsonPost` if `options[''includeFields'']` isn't present), and its action will be used as the URL.

- `Range(min, max)`: This returns an array of values between `min` and `max`. It uses `ko.unwrap` on both the arguments.

- `registerEventHandler(element, eventType, handler)`: This attaches an event handler to the element. It uses jQuery if possible, `addEventListener` if available or `attachEvent` as a last resort (Internet Explorer). If using `attachEvent`, it registers a disposal handler to call `detachEvent`, as IE does not do so automatically.

- `setHtml(node, html)`: This empties the node's contents, unwraps the HTML, and sets the node's HTML using either `jQuery.html`, if available, or `parseHtmlFragement`.

- `stringifyJson(data, replacer, space)`: This uses `ko.unwrap` to handle observable data and calls `JSON.stringify`. The `replacer` and `space` parameters are optional. If the JSON object is not present, it throws an exception.

- `toggleDomNodeCssClass(node, className, shouldHaveClass)`: This uses the `shouldHaveClass` Boolean to either add or remove all of `classNames` Boolean from the node.

- `triggerEvent(element, eventType)`: This triggers the event on the element. It uses jQuery when applicable and handles known issues with raising the click event in IE and in jQuery.

- `unwrapObservable(value)`: This was the original name of `ko.unwrap` and is maintained for backward compatibility. It will either return the underlying value of an observable or the value itself if it's not an observable.

# Summary

While this certainly isn't an exhaustive look at the guts of Knockout, which you probably wouldn't want anyway, you should at least have a good understanding of how Knockout gets most of the important things done. This chapter covered dependency tracking, the *prototype* (`fn`) chain, the binding expression parser, how `ko.applyBindings` works, how Knockout handles templates, and the `ko.utils` namespace. Hopefully, you will feel comfortable with how each of these systems work internally. Knowing how these pieces fit together should help you in troubleshooting those really tricky bugs.

# Index

containerless syntax, with custom bindings
about 70, 71
virtual elements API, using 71-73
Content Security Policy (CSP) 230
control flow bindings
about 22
foreach binding 25, 26
if binding 23
with binding 24
CRUD (Create, Read, Update, Delete) 36
currying 164
custom binding handlers
using 48
custom binding providers 84-91
custom component loaders 113
custom configurations
components, loading with 116
custom dialogs
about 145-148
alternative method 148, 149
custom elements
registering 115
custom loader
registering 115
custom modal dialogs
about 180-182
default context, replacing 183

# D

data-bind attribute 18
data binding pattern 45-47
data bindings
components, combining with 112
data-bind syntax
about 18
binding, against functions 20
binding, with expressions 20
binding, with function expressions 21
binding, with nested properties 19
ko.toJSON, used for debugging 22
parentheses, using in bindings 21
data-part attributes
used, for modifying Durandal
widgets 157, 158

debouncing functions
URL 39
default loader 114, 115
default message 202
define method
about 99
dependencies parameter 99
module function parameter 99
module name parameter 99
dependencies
registering 220
subscribing to 221, 222
dependency tracking
about 217
ko.dependencyDetection module 218-220
descendant bindings
about 64
controlling 65
dirty flag
URL 153
disposal handler 52
DOM
modifying, with bindings 52, 54
DOM local storage
URL 35
domNodeDisposal object
methods 239
Durandal
overview 128-131
promises 128
URL, for documentation 128
dynamic child routes 179, 180
dynamic namespaced bindings 92, 93
dynamic templates 28

# E

embedded Ruby syntax interpolation
adding 83
embedded text bindings 91
environment setup
about 8
JavaScript's compatibility 9
samples of code, viewing 9

## V

validationElement binding  202
validator function  202
view caching, advanced composition  173
view, composition option  136
view, Contacts List application
  about  41
  contacts list  42, 43
  edit form  41, 42
view locations  137, 138
viewmodel
  defining  16
  issues, with prototypes  17
  preparing, with activate  150-152
  self keyword  16
  serializing  18
  this keyword  16
  updating  204
  versus model  39
viewmodel, MVVM pattern
  about  191
  cluttering  192, 193

viewmodel registration
  about  108
  AMD module used  109
  constructor function  108
  factory function  109
  singleton object  108
view, MVVM pattern
  about  191
  cluttering  193, 194
viewpath strings, composition option  135
virtual template nodes
  closing  79, 80

## W

widgets, Durandal
  about  155
  creating  155, 156
  modifying, with data-part
    attributes  157, 158
  using  156, 157
Windows Presentation
  Foundation (WPF)  10
with binding  24
writable computed observables  13

## Thank you for buying
# Mastering KnockoutJS

# About Packt Publishing

Packt, pronounced 'packed', published its first book "*Mastering phpMyAdmin for Effective MySQL Management*" in April 2004 and subsequently continued to specialize in publishing highly focused books on specific technologies and solutions.

Our books and publications share the experiences of your fellow IT professionals in adapting and customizing today's systems, applications, and frameworks. Our solution based books give you the knowledge and power to customize the software and technologies you're using to get the job done. Packt books are more specific and less general than the IT books you have seen in the past. Our unique business model allows us to bring you more focused information, giving you more of what you need to know, and less of what you don't.

Packt is a modern, yet unique publishing company, which focuses on producing quality, cutting-edge books for communities of developers, administrators, and newbies alike. For more information, please visit our website: www.packtpub.com.

# About Packt Open Source

In 2010, Packt launched two new brands, Packt Open Source and Packt Enterprise, in order to continue its focus on specialization. This book is part of the Packt Open Source brand, home to books published on software built around Open Source licenses, and offering information to anybody from advanced developers to budding web designers. The Open Source brand also runs Packt's Open Source Royalty Scheme, by which Packt gives a royalty to each Open Source project about whose software a book is sold.

# Writing for Packt

We welcome all inquiries from people who are interested in authoring. Book proposals should be sent to author@packtpub.com. If your book idea is still at an early stage and you would like to discuss it first before writing a formal book proposal, contact us; one of our commissioning editors will get in touch with you.

We're not just looking for published authors; if you have strong technical skills but no writing experience, our experienced editors can help you develop a writing career, or simply get some additional reward for your expertise.

**open source**
community experience distilled

# KnockoutJS Starter

ISBN: 978-1-78216-114-1       Paperback: 50 pages

Learn how to knock out your next app in no time with KnockoutJS

1. Learn something new in an instant!
   A short, fast, focused guide that delivers immediate results.

2. Learn how to develop a deployable app as the author walks you through each step.

3. Understand how to customize and extend KnockoutJS to take your app to the next level.

4. Great examples that show how KnockoutJS can simplify your code and make it more robust.

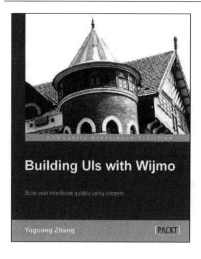

# Building UIs with Wijmo

ISBN: 978-1-84969-606-7       Paperback: 116 pages

Build user interfaces quickly using widgets

1. Learn to configure Wijmo components for common usage scenarios.

2. Build adaptive websites that work on desktops and mobile devices.

3. Integrate Wijmo with Knockout to develop real-time applications.

Please check **www.PacktPub.com** for information on our titles

## jQuery HOTSHOT

ISBN: 978-1-84951-910-6    Paperback: 296 pages

Ten practical projects that exercise your skill, build your confidence, and help you master jQuery

1. See how many of jQuery's methods and properties are used in real situations. Covers jQuery 1.9.

2. Learn to build jQuery from source files, write jQuery plugins, and use jQuery UI and jQuery Mobile.

3. Familiarize yourself with the latest related technologies such as HTML5, CSS3, and frameworks such as Knockout.js.

## Real-time Web Application Development using Vert.x 2.0

ISBN: 978-1-78216-795-2    Paperback: 122 pages

An intuitive guide to building applications for the real-time web with the Vert.x platform

1. Get started with developing applications for the real-time Web.

2. From concept to deployment, learn the full development workflow of a real-time web application.

3. Utilize the Java skills you already have while stepping up to the next level.

Please check **www.PacktPub.com** for information on our titles

Printed in Great Britain
by Amazon